HANK GREENBERG

Hank Greenberg

The Hero Who Didn't Want to Be One

MARK KURLANSKY

Yale
UNIVERSITY
PRESS

New Haven and London

Frontispiece: Hank Greenberg at home in the Bronx with his brother Joe, Joe's wife, Marilyn, and their mother, Sarah, February 27, 1941, just before Hank was inducted into the army. Copyright © Bettmann/CORBIS.

Yale University Press books may be purchased in quantity for educational, business, or promotional use. For information, please e-mail sales.press@yale.edu (U.S. office) or sales@yaleup.co.uk (U.K. office).

Set in Janson type by Vonda's Comp Services, Comstock Park, Michigan.
Printed in the United States of America.

Library of Congress Cataloging-in-Publication Data
Kurlansky, Mark.
Hank Greenberg : the hero who didn't want to be one / Mark Kurlansky.
p.   cm. — (Jewish lives)
Includes bibliographical references and index.
ISBN 978-0-300-13660-9 (cloth : alk. paper)   1. Greenberg, Hank.
2. Baseball players—United States—Biography.   3. Detroit Tigers
(Baseball team)   4. Jews—Sports—United States—Biography.   I. Title.
GV865.G68K87 2010
796.357092—dc22
[B]   2010044279

A catalogue record for this book is available from the British Library.

This paper meets the requirements of ANSI/NISO Z39.48-1992
(Permanence of Paper).

10 9 8 7 6 5 4 3 2 1

BOOKS BY MARK KURLANSKY

A Continent of Islands: Searching for the Caribbean Destiny
A Chosen Few: The Resurrection of European Jewry
Cod: A Biography of the Fish That Changed the World
The Basque History of the World: The Story of a Nation
The White Man in the Tree and Other Stories
Salt: A World History
1968: The Year That Rocked the World
Boogaloo on 2nd Avenue: A Novel of Pastry, Guilt, and Music
Nonviolence: The History of a Dangerous Idea
The Big Oyster: History on the Half Shell
The Last Fish Tale: The Fate of the Atlantic and Survival
    in Gloucester, America's Oldest Fishing Port and
    Most Original Town
The Food of a Younger Land: A Portrait of American Food—
    before the National Highway System, before Chain
    Restaurants, and before Frozen Food, when the Nation's
    Food Was Seasonal, Regional, and Traditional—from the
    Lost WPA Files
The Eastern Stars: How Baseball Changed the Dominican
    Town of San Pedro de Macorís
Edible Stories: A Novel in Sixteen Parts

דימ‍ת טאָה סאָוו לוויף, לדנעמ רעטאָף, ןײמ ראָף ןוא טמאַטש יז ןענאָוו ווף
טינ טסעגנראָף סאָוו ןאיראָמ ראָף, רצטולאָסבא רצד לאָמ סקצז זיא לאָב, א
קידוצ ןוא ןיה ןֿפראַו ןיא דיז ןליֿפש ןשטנעמ יו ןעו זא טנימעג סומיסקאָמ.

───────────────

To Marian, who always remembers where she came from, and to my father,
Phillip Mendel, who thought a game of catch had a six-throw maximum.

I am burdened with the truck and chimera, hope,
acquired in the sweating sick-excited passage
   in steerage, strange and estranged
     —Delmore Schwartz, "America, America!"

CONTENTS

WHO WAS Hank Greenberg? He was a baseball player who hit a lot of home runs before most of us were born. Babe Ruth, by the record book, was a better hitter, others were better fielders, but Greenberg was indisputably one of the greats of baseball history, winning games with dazzling bravado in late innings. Yet what is most important about this man, what made him a legend, is not how far and how often he hit the ball; it is that Hank Greenberg showed a humanity and strength of character far beyond that of most sports heroes.

His was a profoundly American story, one that many know well from their own families—the struggle for a better life, to transcend the world of his immigrant parents. And his was a good Jewish story—the Jew who fans and the press insisted stood up for the Jewish people, and yet a man who called his Jewishness "an accident of birth" and did not engage in a single religious practice.

If it is true, as Ralph Waldo Emerson wrote in 1841, that "there is no history, only biography," what place does the life of Hank Greenberg hold? It is a small but significant chapter in the story of humanity's struggle to overcome narrow-minded prejudice, to rise above bigotry. What matters is not that Hank Greenberg stood up for the Jewish people, it is that he stood up for all people. In 1949, responding to a letter from a Philadelphia doctor who had written him about the chances of a Jewish boy making it to the major leagues, Greenberg said all the right things about working hard and about baseball's blindness to any attributes but talent. With a touch of modern political incorrectness he declared: "No one cares whether the player is a Hindu, a Chinaman or a Jew." He signed off. But then, as an afterthought to the dictated letter typed by a secretary, he wrote in his own hand at the bottom, "If prejudice does exist, and I refuse to recognize that it does, then let it spur you on to greater achievement rather than accept it and be licked by it."

This is important advice for Jews, blacks, Asians, Latinos, women, gays, lesbians—anyone who is faced with people who hate them or want to hold them back. It was not a unique point of view. Others, especially African American writers from the novelist Ralph Ellison to President Barack Obama, have expressed similar points of view. But Greenberg expressed it early and with both persistence and eloquence, using his standing to influence Jews and, by extension, other minorities.

As a player, Hank Greenberg faced haters every day, as did Jackie Robinson a few years later. But it is not that Greenberg was the Jewish Jackie Robinson or Robinson the black Hank Greenberg. They were two men whose performance in the public eye was exemplary and remains meaningful to this day.

It is not polite to talk about it, but in America there has often been a competition over victimhood between blacks and Jews. As the Warsaw Jewish writer Konstanty Gebert said, speaking about the tension between Poles and Jews over the memory of Auschwitz, "On the pinnacle of suffering there is room for just one." History has not accorded Greenberg the full credit he deserves because the abuse of Jews in baseball has been eclipsed by the abuse of blacks. After all, Jews were never banned from the major leagues and forced to play in Jewish leagues. And the abuse of blacks in baseball continued far longer. Yes, Greenberg encountered innumerable incidents of anti-Semitism in his ballplaying career, especially when he went after Babe Ruth's single-season home run record in 1938, but much fresher in the memory of fans is the mountain of threatening racist mail with the salutation "Dear Nigger" that Hank Aaron received as he pursued Ruth's career home run record in 1973.

To his credit, Greenberg never aspired to the pinnacle of suffering. He often said that Robinson endured far worse abuse than he did. Greenberg hated prejudice in all its forms. He believed that his stance was not against anti-Semitism but against the ignorant bigots of the world; he recognized that his persecutors and Robinson's were often the same people.

When Greenberg started his baseball career, there were few examples to follow; he had no idea what he was about to face. He was a true pioneer, finding his way as he went along, learning from mistakes, but showing remarkable courage, discipline, and restraint. To maintain stature and dignity in the face of abuse calls for enormous grace. The Jewish slugger's pioneering stance—he had been fending off public attacks of blatant bigotry for more than a decade—was the approach Dodgers management instructed Robinson to adopt in dealing with harassment. The Cleveland Indians, with Greenberg as part of the management team, gave similar instructions to the second African American brought into the majors, Larry Doby. Robinson and Doby responded with remarkable courage, discipline, and restraint. No one in either organization ever credited Greenberg with the strategy, but he had provided an example that was well known to all of baseball.

The real importance to history of Greenberg's hitting or the brilliant base running of Jackie Robinson is simply that those skills put them in front of the public. Once there, not only did they show physical courage, grit, determination, and poise under pressure—in baseball terms, clutch—but they showed moral character. We want our athletes to be "heroes," possibly the most overused word in the English language. But how often do they show moral character? Most who truly achieve this stature have been tested by the times in which they played.

Hank Greenberg was a Jewish star in the 1930s. In a different decade he probably would have been just a great ballplayer, which was all he ever wanted to be. He defended Jews by defending himself, but he never wanted to be defined that way. His whole life was a struggle to move beyond what he saw as a confining tribalism. A good-natured man with little angst, he sometimes laughed and sometimes protested, but he never accepted the definition of himself that some of his Jewish fans had cut out for him. Among these fans, some even today insist that it was anti-Semitism that stopped him from beating Babe Ruth's home run record; they stand without knowing it in complete opposition to what Hank Greenberg was about. It was a central drama of his life that some of his Jewish fans could never quite accept who Hank Greenberg really was.

Only at the end of his life did Greenberg recognize that this special role for Jews was a positive thing. He never used anti-Semitism as an excuse because he understood that to do so would diminish him, that the people who hated him wanted to make him small, that if he could just keep his composure, they would be the ones to shrink. That is an inspiring idea, an example of how to defeat bigotry, and it is why Hank Greenberg, all six foot four of him, was a giant.

HANK GREENBERG

Prologue

———◆◦◆◦◆———

The One Holy Day

The true value of a human being is determined
primarily by the measure and the sense in which
he has attained liberation from the self.
—Albert Einstein, *Mein Weltbild* (My Worldview)

IN 1934 Hank Greenberg observed Yom Kippur, possibly
for the only time in his adult life. It defined him for the rest of
his days, though this was not at all what he had wanted. To him
it seemed absurd to be defined by his religious observance
when he was utterly unobservant.

In the early 1930s the Detroit Tigers had emerged from
years of mediocrity to become a contending baseball team in
the American League. The Tigers had accomplished this with
an infield that is still remembered as one of the best hitting
combinations in the history of the game. Between Greenberg
on first base, Charlie Gehringer on second, Billy Rogell at short-

stop, and Marv Owen on third, the Tiger infield got 769 hits in the 1934 season, 201 of them by Greenberg alone. The only better hitter was Gehringer, who batted just in front of him. If Gehringer could get on base, Greenberg could drive him in, which was why Greenberg led the team in runs batted in, with 139.

Though Greenberg was not a great first baseman, the toss from Rogell to Gehringer and the relay to Greenberg made the trio a famous double play combination. Ballplayers spend long hours together perfecting this kind of play, and few achieve it with the Tigers' consistency.

Furthermore, with a core of left fielder Goose Goslin, Greenberg, and Gehringer—affectionately known to Detroit fans as "the G-men"—Detroit's lineup was said to be unstoppable.

It is so difficult to hit a pitch from a major league pitcher that anyone who succeeds one out of every three times he bats, a batting average of .333, is considered exceptionally good. In fact, an average over .300 is considered the mark of a star batter. Greenberg hit .301 in 1933, and in 1934, he was doing even better. He would end the season with a stellar .339 batting average.

By the fall of 1934 the Detroit Tigers were on track to win their first pennant in twenty-five years, and Hank Greenberg was at the center of that accomplishment. The baseball fans of Detroit had been waiting a long time for this victory and they were hungry for it. But the Jews of America had a different kind of hunger. That is why in the 154-game season of 1934, while Gehringer, Rogell, and Owen played every game, Greenberg played only 153 and ended up famous for the one he didn't play.

Because the lunar calendar of Judaism does not match the solar calendar of Christianity, which baseball follows, the Jewish holidays fall differently on the baseball schedule from season to season. The Jewish high holidays, Rosh Hashanah and

Yom Kippur, come between early September and late October. This means that they may fall harmlessly before the pennant race comes down to the last few crucial games or, before the season was lengthened in the 1960s, after the World Series. But on occasion the holidays have coincided with the dramatic homestretch of a pennant race or have come during a World Series.

Before 1969, when annual postseason playoff series were instituted, the team with the best record in the American League played in the World Series against the team with the best record in the National League. The competition for the top slot, symbolized by the pennant, could become intense in the last weeks of a season. Some of the classic pennant races were between the two New York National League teams, the Dodgers and Giants. But in 1934 it was the American League that was engaged in a race down to the wire, between the Tigers and the Yankees.

In truth it was not as tight a race as that year's National League contest between the Cardinals and the Giants. That race illustrated how quickly things could turn. As of Labor Day, the Giants were a comfortable six games ahead, but the Cardinals had caught up to them by the following week and eventually beat them by two games. The 1934 Cardinals, led by a pitching staff of Dizzy Dean and his brother Paul, became one of the most remarkable teams in baseball history. Dizzy won 30 games that season, reaching a plateau attained only once since, in 1968, when Denny McLain won 31 for Detroit. The 1934 Cardinals were so rough and scruffy that they were called the Gashouse Gang, for a famous Manhattan street gang. Ironically, the Gashouse Gang came with its own religious issue. The team's general manager, Branch Rickey, was a devout Methodist who disapproved of playing on the Sabbath and refused to watch Sunday games.

In the American League's run-up to the pennant, Detroit

was still four games ahead of the Yankees by Rosh Hashanah, and, even though Gehringer and several other big Detroit hitters were slumping, with Babe Ruth declining in his last Yankee season, the Yankees were not likely to catch up. The claim by many fans and some press that Greenberg was absolutely essential to Detroit for that one game of Rosh Hashanah on September 10 was an exaggeration. Even Greenberg seemed to overplay the moment when he said years later that "The team was fighting for first place." Perhaps more candidly, he explained to his son Stephen, with whom he often discussed the events of September 1934, that it was his first season on a contending team and he really wanted to play.

Yet somehow whether or not Hank Greenberg was going to play first base on September 10 became a national issue, one that was written about extensively in the Detroit and the national press. Greenberg, twenty-three years old and in his second full year in the majors, was beginning to recognize that he was somehow more than just a ballplayer. Both Jews and non-Jews were beginning to see him as a kind of national Jew, a symbol.

Greenberg did not say what he was going to do, probably because he hadn't decided, but this only fueled speculation by fans and the press. The press, especially in Detroit and in Boston, whose Red Sox were in town to play the Tigers, worked every angle of this Rosh Hashanah story for a reading public that included many who had never heard of the holiday. Reporters conferred with Jewish religious leaders such as Leo Franklin, a reform rabbi often considered the leading rabbi of Detroit. According to Greenberg and to many other accounts, Franklin, like a good Tigers fan, argued with Talmudic virtuosity that the Jewish New Year was a day of joy and therefore a good ballgame was in order. He even pointed out that sports had been played in the streets of Jerusalem during holy days in Roman times, and only later admitted that only Roman children, not Jews, had participated in those games. Greenberg always said that Rabbi Franklin had given him permission to play. Learning of Franklin's advice, the *Detroit News* ran the headline "Talmud Clears Greenberg for Holiday Play."

But a number of publications of the time quoted Franklin saying something entirely different. He told both the Detroit and Boston newspapers that "in the Jewish faith there is no power granted to the rabbi to give dispensation to anyone for doing anything," and that "we insist on the doctrine of personal responsibility."

Jewish religious authorities know how to argue both sides: Greenberg should not play since he did that for a living and he was not allowed to work on the high holidays, but on the other hand, as Franklin pointed out, it could be argued that he would be playing for the good of others—the team and the community. Greenberg, Rabbi Franklin repeatedly stated, "must decide for himself."

The leading national sports paper of the day, the *Sporting News*, opined that what Franklin was saying was that the Jewish establishment, "The Church," as the paper put it, would not have the right to criticize Greenberg if he decided to play. Of course, the press, like Jews everywhere, could interpret the rabbi in a variety of ways. They could also find different rabbis.

The press and public were beginning to learn that Jews do not have a church with a singular point of view. Jews argue. Joseph Thumin, a leading Detroit Orthodox rabbi, said on the day of the game that it would be perfectly fine for Greenberg to play that day. But there were three conditions. Orthodox Jews could not buy tickets that day; there could be no smoking in the stadium; and all ballpark snacks had to be kosher. The interpretation of Thumin's statement in the Detroit press, both mainstream and in the one English-language Jewish paper, was that Greenberg was free to play.

Other rabbis stated categorically that he should not play, and like-minded Jewish fans throughout the country wrote imploring letters to Greenberg and even called him on the phone. In truth, though, the entire debate was founded on a compromise that Jewish law had already made with America, because to a strictly observant Jew, the most important holiday is neither Rosh Hashanah nor Yom Kippur but Shabbat, the Sabbath, from sundown Friday to sundown Saturday. This is the only holiday whose observance is one of the Ten Commandments. No baseball player has ever refused to play games on Shabbat, and it is doubtful that he could keep his job if he did. But Jewish practice is full of compromises, and by 1934 the debate over playing on Shabbat was long past and the burning question was: should a Jew play a sport—not least, one that would be the focus of national attention—on the two holiest days of the year aside from the Sabbath?

Greenberg was caught between the Jewish world and the baseball world, and there was no way to please everyone, not even to please all Jews. Though seldom observant, this year he went to Detroit's oldest Conservative synagogue, Shaarey Zedek, for Rosh Hashanah. The synagogue was in a grand building, where ushers in formal attire had once shown worshipers to their seats. The Detroit *Jewish Chronicle* reported on his observance in great detail: that he was handed a talith, that he was asked to be one of the bearers of the Torah, that he declined, saying that he was "only a ballplayer." According to some accounts he went to one service, according to others, two. In his own account Greenberg says nothing about having attended Rosh Hashanah services.

Greenberg, who was not known for theatrical stunts, seemed genuinely conflicted right up to game time. He went to Navin Field but did not put on his uniform for batting practice, telling the starting pitcher, Eldon Auker, that he did not know what to do. Auker, who came from rural Kansas, did not know what Rosh Hashanah was, and later claimed that Greenberg was the first Jew he ever met. In any event he knew nothing about Jews and cared little about the subject. He only knew that Greenberg was a great hitter and he wanted him playing on a day when he was pitching. No matter how well you pitch, you cannot win the game unless the team scores runs. So it was with considerable relief that he and the Detroit fans saw Greenberg take his position at first base. He had made up his mind.

Greenberg never regretted that decision, especially since he hit two home runs, the second to win the game in the ninth inning, and the Tigers beat Boston 2–1. A Jewish newspaper in Indianapolis ran a story about him under the headline "The Jewish Babe Ruth." Suddenly Greenberg, playing only his second year in major league baseball, was being compared by press and fans alike to the legendary Babe.

There were jokes everywhere about God's role in Detroit's victory. For a moment even the mainstream Detroit papers seemed to revel in Jewishness, with the *Detroit Free Press* running a jubilant headline that spelled out a New Year's greeting in Hebrew letters, "Lashanah tova, Hank," and another one declaring, "Hank's Homers Are Strictly Kosher." The *Detroit Times* wrote that his batting swing was "propelled by a force born of the desperation and the pride of a young Jew who turned his back on the ancient ways of his race and creed to help his teammates." They described his two home runs as Greenberg's blast on his shofar.

Such comments made Greenberg uneasy, and he confided to third baseman Marv Owen that he did not know whether he could play nine days later on Yom Kippur. Despite the game's outcome, not everyone was pleased with his conduct on Rosh Hashanah. Rabbi Thumin expressed concern about the example he had set by going to services and then going to the ballgame. "Greenberg's violation of Rosh Hashanah was carried out with such success that this left a bad impression on light-minded young Jews," Thumin said. "I caught hell from my fellow parishioners, I caught hell from some rabbis," Greenberg told Owen.

Yom Kippur, the Day of Atonement, unlike the joyous holiday Rosh Hashanah, is a solemn day of fasting and prayer that is so significant in the Jewish religion that it is often observed by secular Jews—so-called Yom Kippur Jews. Greenberg was not even a Yom Kippur Jew. And yet his Jewish observance had become a national issue.

To many nonobservant Jews, quietly ignoring Yom Kippur is acceptable as long as you don't get caught. You don't want to be seen not observing Yom Kippur. In his story "The Search," the great nineteenth-century Yiddish writer Shalom Aleichem described a wealthy man who showed up in town on Yom Kippur looking for a place to fast and pray. He was carrying a great deal of money, and having nowhere to put it he took it with him to the synagogue. While he was enraptured in prayer, the money disappeared; afterward, the rabbi ordered everyone to empty his pockets. One man refused and, convinced that they had found their thief, the worshipers held him down and turned out his pockets. Instead of stolen money, they found freshly gnawed chicken bones and still moist plum pits. The man had preferred to be taken for a thief than to be exposed to the community as having failed to fast on Yom Kippur.

Now here was Greenberg, who neither fasted nor prayed on Yom Kippur, being watched by the entire Jewish community of America. His parents, who had raised him to be observant, and all their friends and neighbors would read in the papers whether he observed the Holy Day or not. It is not an easy thing for a Jew to be seen flouting Yom Kippur by every Jew in America, not to mention non-Jews. When in the past five thousand years had the observance or nonobservance of one holiday by a single Jew attracted this much attention? Greenberg's parents had warned him that being a baseball player would be problematic for a Jew, and suddenly their caution seemed prophetic.

Greenberg had never wanted to be known as the Jewish baseball player. All he wanted to do was play baseball. But it was his lot to play baseball in the most anti-Semitic period in American history, and in times of anti-Semitism, Jews and anti-Semites alike garner attention. Whether he liked it or not, Greenberg was never going to be just a baseball player.

Some papers argued that he should play, some that he should not. But it became clear from the press and the mail and phone calls he was getting that the Gentile world wanted him to play and the Jews of America wanted him to observe Yom Kippur. While the pressure was on from the Jewish community, it was seldom pointed out that Greenberg's Rosh Hashanah home runs had helped take the pennant-race pressure off of the Tigers. The Yom Kippur game was one of eleven left in the regular season for the team, and they had to win just four of them to clinch the American League title. Meanwhile, the Yankees, with their aging Ruth, would have to overcome even greater odds than the Cardinals had faced; even if they won every remaining game, it would probably not be enough. The Tigers could certainly afford a single game without Hank Greenberg on Yom Kippur.

As a result, though there were many articles speculating on Greenberg's next decision, there was less press coverage than there had been ten days earlier. And there was considerably less pressure from fans and Tigers management. Everyone would forgive him for not playing this game, even if the Tigers lost.

Hank did not let down his Jewish fans. The day came and he did not play. Instead, he went to synagogue to observe Yom Kippur. The decision resonated far beyond what he could have imagined: it marked the beginning of the enduring myth of

Hank Greenberg. In baseball terms, he had played the game when he was needed and sat out the game when he was not. But the story is remembered, even by non-Jews, in Jewish terms: he would not play on Yom Kippur. For all his history of timely hits winning games at the last moment, this day on which he did not play is one of the most remembered moments of his career.

The Tigers played without him and they lost the game to the Yankees. But the *New York Times* reported the next morning, September 20, that the Tigers had the pennant practically "signed, sealed and delivered" anyway, and the *Times* reporter was right. Detroit won the pennant comfortably, and went on to play the Cardinals. The World Series was a tight seven-game contest in which the Gashouse Gang lived up to its reputation, with Dizzy Dean's pitching eight innings a day after taking such a forceful throw off his head that according to the press the ball popped thirty feet in the air, and Ducky Medwick sliding into Owen in the final game with his spikes up and then kicking him hard in the crotch. The crowd pelted Medwick with hot dogs and soda bottles until Commissioner Kenesaw Mountain Landis ordered him removed from the game. Despite such antics, the Cardinals won the game and won the Series. Detroit was left broken-hearted, but it was one of the great World Series of all time, a season famous for the Gashouse Gang but equally famous for the big Jewish G-man on first base who had refused to play on Yom Kippur.

On the morning of Yom Kippur, when Greenberg walked into Shaarey Zedek, the packed service came to a halt so that the congregation could give him a standing ovation. Applause in a synagogue on any day of the year is unusual, but especially on the Day of Atonement. But Greenberg was being applauded everywhere, as he had overnight become a hero of the Jewish people. One baseball magazine even compared him to Moses, leading his people to the liberation of assimilation. The assumption among non-Jews was that if Jews could play baseball like Greenberg, they could be "like us," which surely must be their goal. But to Jews on Yom Kippur 1934, he stood for just the opposite—someone who could preserve Jewish tradition by playing baseball *and* going to shul.

Edgar Guest, a nationally syndicated newspaper poet from the *Detroit Free Press*, wrote a poem in honor of Greenberg, which ended:

Come Yom Kippur—holy fast day worldwide over to
    the Jew—
And Hank Greenberg to his teachings and the old tradition
    true
Spent the day among his people and he didn't come to play.
Said Murphy to Mulrooney, "We shall lose the game today!
We shall miss him on the infield and shall miss him at
    the bat,
But he's true to his religion—and I honor him for that!"

All over the country it was reported by the press and repeated by fans, both Jewish and non-Jewish, that Hank Greenberg was "true to his religion," that he stood by his people and understood his responsibility as a Jewish leader. In the Detroit Jewish community, Greenberg's decision to sit out was a huge event that still resonated more than seventy years later. Eliot Sharlit, a Detroit Jew, was four years old in 1934. "I was a little boy but I still remember Yom Kippur when he didn't play and went to Shaarey Zedik." Harriet Coleman, another Detroit Jew who was an eleven-year-old then, recalled that she and other Jewish people felt good about Greenberg's decision "because there was a lot of anti-Semitism in the area at the time." Greenberg was "adopted by the Jewish community," she said. "Families invited him to dinner."

No Jewish sports figure had ever before been put in this position. Later on the day when Greenberg had played on Rosh Hashanah 1934, Barney Ross, born Barnet David Rasofsky, the nearly unbeatable world lightweight and junior welterweight champion who was the first fighter ever to hold two titles at the same time, refused to box on the holy day. Ross was a popular Jewish hero, but few people, even Jewish fans, cared about his decision. It was easy to postpone a fight to another night. Ross had no teammates to disappoint and no season schedule to keep. The press even accused him of changing the date so that he wouldn't lose his fan base for the night of the fight.

After Yom Kippur, the Tiger first baseman came to be seen as a muscular six-foot-four-inch bulwark against anti-Semitism. Fans and reporters started to ignore the real Hank Greenberg in favor of this image of the mythic super-Jew, the deeply religious man who also played baseball very well. As the *Detroit Free Press* saw it, Greenberg "is an orthodox Jew and practices his religion faithfully." Greenberg, a humble but gracious man, tried to avoid the fanfare, turning down a proposed dinner in his honor by the Detroit Jewish community. In fact, many Jews were relieved that he had turned it down, subscribing to the long-standing Jewish belief that it is "bad for the Jews" for any individual Jew to get too much attention, because this draws out the anti-Semites.

Privately, Greenberg, the secular Jew, was both embarrassed and amused by his new image. Years later, he joked with his close friend and business associate Bill Veeck about the bad poem and about the declaration of every Jewish mother, starting with his own, that "he never played on the holidays." This made him chortle. "I ate out a lot on that one. They always said, 'He never would play on the high holidays.' I only had one chance!" Then he would burst into loud contagious laughter because Hank loved to laugh and often smothered his punch lines. Even today it is often said that Hank Greenberg would never play on Yom Kippur. But the only other time a critical game for him fell on Yom Kippur was the following year during the World Series. Greenberg made clear his intention to play, but he was unable to because of a wrist injury.

In a 1934 article in the *New York Evening Post*, Hank's father voiced his opinion about his son's decision not to play on Yom Kippur, asserting, "We are an orthodox family." He said that when they saw their son on the Tigers' last East Coast trip, Hank had promised not to play on Rosh Hashanah or Yom Kippur. He had apologized to his parents for the Rosh Hashanah game but explained that the manager, Mickey Cochrane, had pressured him into playing. "Henry could not refuse very well," his father explained to the *Post*. But his father added that Yom Kippur was different: "I put my foot down and Henry obeyed."

Was it as simple as that? Twenty-three-year-old Hank Greenberg did not play on Yom Kippur because his father told him it was forbidden? Hank's son Steve said, "He really fretted about it because he wanted to play. . . . If his parents had been dead or he had no family, he clearly would have played. But I think out of respect for his parents and the notoriety [the situation] was getting, he decided not to play." Steve Greenberg continued, "That Edgar Guest poem, 'We shall miss him on the infield, and shall miss him at the bat/But he's true to his religion and we honor him for that'—that is the myth. The truth is he desperately wanted to play. It was his life's passion."

Hank Greenberg had been anointed a sports hero, and when fans in the 1930s anointed a sports hero, they often gave him an affectionate nickname. Benny Leonard, the great lightweight boxing champion who, until Greenberg, was the biggest sports hero in Jewish America, had been dubbed by Jewish fans "The Great Bennah." In this tradition, Jewish fans started calling Hank Greenberg "Hankus Pankus," a name probably invented by the Tigers' radio announcer Ty Tysom, but which fell in line with the rhyming gags of Yiddish humor of the time. It made him their own. Now Hankus Pankus was theirs too.

There had already been an estimated thirty-five Jewish players in the major leagues by the time Greenberg played his first major league game in 1930. Nor was he alone during his career. Twenty-two other Jewish players started major league careers in the 1930s, during Greenberg's best years. But for the fans, Jewish baseball begins with Hank Greenberg. He was the first important Jewish player, the first Jewish baseball star. Like all Jewish players, simply by playing baseball he was by definition a symbol of successful assimilation, but now, because he refused to play on Yom Kippur, he was also a symbol of a refusal to assimilate—a paradox that did not seem to puzzle his fans.

Greenberg fans often said proudly, "He was the first player not to change his name." If by this they meant his surname, it should be noted that two Cohens, an Arnovich, a Berg, a Berman, two Mayers, a Meyer, a Rosenberg, a Rosenthal, a Schwarz, and a Solomon all preceded him. If his fans meant that Greenberg hadn't changed his name at all, they were wrong. Julius Wolk, who grew up with Greenberg in the Bronx, said, "Hank? Hank? When we were little kids everyone called him Hymie, family and friends. He was known as Hymie in P.S. 44." He was still Hyman Greenberg, the name his parents gave him upon his birth, in early New York newspaper reports of the promising young player. It was in Detroit in the early 1930s, as he became a major leaguer, that he became Hank and eventually Henry, then Henry Benjamin Greenberg, the name that appears on his Hall of Fame plaque. (Shortly before he died, Greenberg surprised his family with the confession that he had made up his middle name. He had done it so that he would have three initials on his luggage like the other players did. So he took his brother Ben's name as a middle name.)

To his die-hard Jewish fans, it was unthinkable that Hank Greenberg would have changed his name for purposes of assimilation. But Morris Barret, formerly Morris Berkowitz, who was fifteen years Greenberg's junior, remembered him differently. Berkowitz played baseball for James Monroe High School in the Bronx, Greenberg's old school. A promising left-handed hitter, Berkowitz was the team captain, and Greenberg used to like to come by the baseball field when he was visiting his parents, to give Berkowitz advice. Sometimes they joked around in Yiddish. Hank would advise him on hitting. "Berky, don't swing at every pitch like you're going to hit a home run. Just hit the ball." But his most important advice, according to Morris, was, "Berky, if you are going to play professional baseball, change your name. Don't go through what I went through. I went through hell, especially the first year."

Berkowitz signed with the Yankee organization for $250 a month and $7 daily expenses when on the road. Playing in Class B in Sunbury, Pennsylvania, he was still Morris Berkowitz. When he walked to the plate the fans would shout, "Here comes the Jew Boy." After a number of anti-Semitic incidents, he thought hard about Greenberg's advice, and although he quit after one year to go to college, when he was moved up to Class A and AA teams he played as Sandy Barrett.

The mythical Hank Greenberg had been created at the end of his second year in the majors, just as he was finding his stride as a leading player. Greenberg never sought to be an important Jew. Rather, he wanted to be an important baseball player, and he worked ceaselessly from early boyhood to attain that goal. But even as he spent endless hours in batting practice perfecting his swing and his timing, he learned how complicated it was to be a Jewish sports hero, or, as he preferred to think of himself, a sports hero who is Jewish. And surely this was made even more complicated by the times in which he played ball.

1

Jewish Hitting

"For my part, your *pitzers* and *catzers* may all lie in
the earth. A nice entertainment, indeed! Just like
little children—playing ball! And yet people say
America is a *smart* country. I don't see it."
"'F *caush* you don't, *becaush* you are a bedraggled
greenhorn, afraid to budge out of Heshter Shtreet."
—Abraham Cahan, *Yekl: A Tale of the New York Ghetto*

ONE ANTI-SEMITIC stereotype of a Jew historically popular
among non-Jews is expressed in the slang Polish pejorative
jojne. The jojne is a Jew as a physically weak coward. He will not
fight and he cannot play sports. Jews, not surprisingly, reject
this stereotype, which is why they loved Hank Greenberg's
ability to disprove it. But Jews have tended to buy into a positive version of this image, believing that their natural role is in
intellectual pursuits, not physical ones. To the traditional and

observant Jew, sports interfered with Torah and Talmud studies. For the modern assimilated Jew, sports may interfere with medical studies or law school, or some other form of study leading to a successful career. Both views agree, however, that a Jew has too good a mind to be wasting time on sports. In addition, immigrants such as Greenberg's parents wanted their children to build their careers and make America work for them. To them, sports would lead nowhere fast.

In reality, many Jews have recognized no division between sports and intellectualism. The Jewish writers who have contributed substantially to baseball literature include Chaim Potok, Philip Roth, Bernard Malamud, Robert Pinsky, Nelson Algren, and Irwin Shaw, among many others. Even Jewish writers who didn't choose baseball as a primary subject found it useful as a metaphor. Saul Bellow invoked baseball to explain the character of Humboldt in *Humboldt's Gift*. Delmore Schwartz's character Faber Gottschalk, the dentist in the story "The Statues," loves major league baseball for what it teaches him about partisanship. "To be truly a spectator, however, is a great deal," Schwartz writes, "for it involves the most intense partisanship, a life of the emotions which is at the mercy of success and defeat every day." Mordecai Richler, in his novel *St. Urbain's Horseman*, has his group of expatriate filmmakers in London get together every Sunday for softball in Hampstead Heath.

And it was not only writers who were drawn to the subject of baseball. In 1934, when Roosevelt's New Deal commissioned artists to paint murals of American life, Morris Kantor, born in Minsk in 1896 and raised in the lower Manhattan garment trade, chose as a subject one of the early night baseball games. It became an iconic WPA painting, now part of the collection of the Smithsonian American Art Museum.

In the America of Greenberg's time, baseball had become part of Jewish intellectual and cultural life.

Nor are physical fitness and sports in any way un-Jewish concepts. Zionism, which encouraged the development of a kind of Jewish machismo, helped drive the connection between Jews and sports. The "new Jew"—proud, strong, and athletic—was a frequent subject at Zionist conferences in the late nineteenth and early twentieth centuries. American Jews were to be proud of their Judaism and to express that pride in athleticism. Greenberg, of course, had exceptional talent, but the fact that he was an athletic Jew with a great love of sports was not unusual.

Physical fitness has always been emphasized in Jewish law and studies, going back to ancient times. In the Talmud, Jewish men are instructed that they have a duty to teach three things to their sons: Torah, a trade, and swimming. Often the question is asked, why swimming, and there have been great rabbinical discussions on the subject. Is it a reminder that the Egyptians who could not swim drowned when the parted Red Sea closed? There is in any case general agreement on the overriding point, that physical fitness is crucial to well-being.

Characters from the Bible such as Samson and David show that Jews with physical strength and athletic ability were admired in biblical times. In the twelfth century of the Common Era, the importance of physical fitness was promoted by Maimonides, the great Jewish philosopher and private physician to Sultan Saladin of Egypt. "The health and well-being of the body," he wrote, "is part of one's service of God."

By the late sixteenth century most Jewish leaders held that Jews were forbidden to play sports on the Sabbath, which made it difficult for them to participate in such games as bowling with Christians. Other sports, such as tennis, were for aristocrats and would not have been open to Jews in any event. To many religious Jews, this position on sports on the Sabbath has remained sacrosanct. And so sports became a *goyish* thing, or a defining mark of assimilation.

In the late eighteenth and the nineteenth century, British Jews were assimilated to the point that there were numerous Jewish sports stars. Among the first were the boxers that came out of Aldgate, a Sephardic Jewish slum in London's East End. The most famous was Daniel Mendoza, born in 1764. Mendoza is remembered as the father of "scientific boxing," which included such strategies as jabbing, feinting, blocking, and sidestepping punches. Though it resembles contemporary boxing, in eighteenth-century London it was referred to as the Jewish school of boxing, the implication being that it was a cowardly enterprise.

The most famous nineteenth-century Jewish boxer in America was Joe Choynski, known to fans as Chrysanthemum Joe, Little Joe, or the California Terror. Choynski's parents came from Poland and settled in San Francisco, where Joe was born in 1868. His father, Isidore Nathan Choynski, was one of the first Jews to go to Yale. Isidore was a San Francisco intellectual who owned a bookstore and published a leftist newspaper, the *Public Opinion*. The paper had a reputation for exposing anti-Semitism and venality in high places. When Joe was growing up, literary luminaries like Mark Twain were guests in his home.

Given this background, Isidore was surprisingly accepting of his son's decision to become a professional boxer. He equated Joe's fighting career with his own scrappy career fighting anti-Semitism. The California Terror was a brutal puncher, and though he never got a title bout, he fought champions, two of whom, James J. Jeffries and James J. Corbett, said he was the hardest hitter they ever faced. Though he never beat either of those title holders, he regularly won bouts against larger opponents. Isidore liked the way his son, at 176 pounds much smaller than most heavyweights, destroyed anti-Semitic stereotypes by taking on and defeating big Irish heavyweights.

Many German Jews belonged to German-American sports clubs, which produced numerous Jewish athletes. One of the most notable of these was Lon Myers, a German Jew who emerged from New York City's sports clubs to become the best sprinter of the nineteenth century, a kind of Babe Ruth of short- and middle-distance running. During his twenty-one-year career, Myers held the American record for every race from the fifty-yard dash to the one-mile run. He also held many world records, as well as both the Canadian and the British championships. Myers ran more quarter-miles in under fifty seconds and more half-miles in under two minutes than the combined total of all of the other amateurs and professionals competing at the time.

Long before Greenberg, Jews from western European backgrounds had a considerable impact on baseball. In fact, Lipman Pike, one of the first professional baseball players, was Jewish. Pike was born in 1845 to a Dutch Jewish family that lived in Brooklyn. There were five children and four brothers, three of whom played baseball. All three were left-handed, then as now a much sought-after commodity in baseball. The oldest brother, Boaz, played for a team in the 1850s. Later Lipman and Boaz played together for the Atlantics, a celebrated Brooklyn team. Boaz did not achieve great fame as a player, nor did their younger brother, Jacob or Jay, but Lip Pike became a star.

At the time that Boaz and Lipman were playing for the Atlantics, baseball was still an amateur sport. But in 1866 the Philadelphia Athletics, liking what they saw of Lipman, offered him $20 a week to come to Philadelphia and play third base.

There were at least two other players paid the same fee by the Athletics, and several players on other teams were also rumored to be receiving money, but Pike is remembered as the first paid player, perhaps because he was one of the best. His pay became notorious, even inspiring a legal challenge, which failed. The fact that Pike and his teammates were paid to play had an enormous impact on baseball. Soon many teams had a few top paid players, and by 1869, the first fully professional baseball team, the Cincinnati Red Stockings, had been organized. The Reds went on to win nearly sixty games in a row, which helped to establish professional baseball.

That Lipman Pike was one of the first home run–slugging stars of baseball had long been forgotten when the next Jewish slugging champion, Hank Greenberg, came along. Pike hit home runs in clusters, as if he couldn't miss once he locked in on the pitcher. Nineteenth-century games, played without gloves and with pitching rules that favored offense, often had enormous scores. Still, it was unprecedented when on July 16, 1866, Lipman Pike hit six home runs in a single game, five of them in consecutive at-bats. Today that record remains untouched.

The Pikes were not the lone Jews of early baseball. James Roseman of Brooklyn, an outfielder, played most of his seven-year career with the New York Metropolitans; Joseph "Dutch" Strauss, a Cincinnati-born outfielder, played for three teams in the mid-1880s; Earl "Ike" Samuels, an Illinois-born infielder, played for St. Louis in 1895; and Jake Goodman, from Lancaster, Pennsylvania, was the Milwaukee Cream Citys' regular first baseman in 1878. Other Jewish players had briefer major league careers: Julius Freeman pitched and lost one game for St. Louis in 1888, and Leo Fishel did the same for the New York Giants in 1899. Bill Cristall, born in the Ukraine, pitched a shutout for his sole victory for the 1901 Cleveland Blues. The only other Ukrainian-born major leaguers in baseball history were also Jewish: Reuben Cohen, who changed his last name to Ewing when he played three games for the St. Louis Cardinals in 1921, and pitcher Izzy Goldstein, who won three games pitching for the Detroit Tigers in 1932, the year before they brought Greenberg up from the minors.

And then there was Johnny Kling, one of the best catchers of his era, a leader of the Chicago Cubs team that won four pennants and two World Series between 1906 and 1910. Some historians list the Kansas City–born Kling, whose name may have been Kline originally, as one of the all-time greatest Jewish baseball players; others argue that he was not Jewish at all. Kling avoided commenting on the subject, but after he died, his wife asserted that he was a Baptist. Later she changed the story, saying that he was a Lutheran. Kling's grandson, also named John Kling, insisted that his grandfather was a Jew and turned up membership records in a Kansas City synagogue. Kling also had an older brother, William, who was a ballplayer. The *Encyclopedia of Jews in Sports* includes both Kling brothers, but the *Baseball Almanac* does not list them as Jewish players, nor does the American Jewish Historical Society.

It could be that the Klings were attempting to avoid anti-Semitism the same way Greenberg told Berkowitz to avoid it. But there were not a lot of reported incidents of anti-Semitism in the early days of baseball, and few players at the time concealed their Jewishness. The St. Louis Browns' star pitcher in the first decade of the twentieth century, Barney Pelty, proudly billed himself as "the Yiddish curver."

In the late nineteenth century a number of wealthy German-Jewish businessmen bought ball clubs or shares of them as a badge of their Americanness. One of these was Andrew Freedman, a native New Yorker who owned the New

York Giants from 1895 to 1902. Freedman claimed to have been mistreated by anti-Semitic fellow owners in negotiations on scheduling and other baseball matters. In fact, he was disliked because of his involvement as a backer of the corrupt Tammany Hall political machine that ran New York City with the support of immigrants, especially the Irish. One of the few incidents of anti-Semitism on the nineteenth-century ball field occurred during an 1898 game between the Baltimore Orioles and the Giants at the Polo Grounds, and Freedman was the target. Ducky Holmes, an outfielder for Baltimore who had played the previous season with the Giants, was being harassed before the game by his former teammates. He responded, "Well, I'm glad I'm not working for a sheeny any more." Freedman heard the slur and demanded that the umpire throw Holmes out of the game for using unacceptable language. The umpire said that he hadn't heard anything, whereupon Freedman ordered his players off the field, announced that he was forfeiting the game, and returned the ticketholders' money. But anti-Semitism was not regarded as an important issue in baseball, and the incident was generally noted as further evidence of Freedman's irascible personality.

On March 13, 1881, Tsar Alexander II was killed in St. Petersburg by a bomb tossed by a member of a revolutionary group attempting to overthrow tsarist rule. In the wake of these events, pogroms broke out, and this violence, coupled with widespread poverty, resulted in the emigration of some two million Jews to the United States.

Many of these *ostjuden*, eastern European Jews, settled into urban slums like Manhattan's Lower East Side, lived in poverty, dressed peculiarly, spoke what others believed was a crude, low form of German—Yiddish—and didn't seem to know how to act like Americans. The arrival of this new Jewish population was accompanied by a marked growth in American anti-Semitism, which some in the Jewish establishment blamed on the new immigrants themselves.

The best thing to do, many old-line American Jews reasoned, was to help these people to assimilate. The majority of these new immigrants came from small towns, or were newcomers in eastern European cities for whom fitting into America meant becoming American urbanites. The change, inevitably, took hold more effectively with their children than with the immigrants themselves, creating a tremendous divide between generations. For young people, Hank Greenberg included, baseball was one way to leave the shtetl behind and become a polished city person.

Most first-generation immigrants dreaded remaining "a greenhorn," *di grine* in Yiddish; the ideal was *oysgrinen zikh*, to leave greenhorn ways, to at least become a "yellow," which was a little less green. Yellows still primarily spoke Yiddish, but they threw in an occasional word of English—*greenhorn, di job, di pants, hello, goodbye,* and *loafer,* this last term being used, for example, to describe people who spent their time playing baseball. To help immigrants from eastern Europe and their children better fit in, Jewish aid societies and educational programs were established, along with sports centers. In the 1870s a wave of anti-Semitism in America had caused most athletic associations to start excluding Jews. The creation of Jewish sporting clubs was an obvious response.

One of the earliest and most important Jewish athletic centers was the Young Men's Hebrew Association (YMHA), loosely modeled after the Young Men's Christian Association (YMCA). Originally founded in Baltimore in 1854 as a social club intended to encourage Jewish values, the YMHA provided an opportunity for young German Jews to socialize and play sports. The discussion and promotion of literature was also an important aspect of the first YMHA. In the next two decades, more than twenty YMHAs sprung up in urban German-Jewish neighborhoods. New York's YMHA was started in 1874 by German Jews on West 24th Street and included a reading room and a gymnasium.

Part of the mission, at the YMHAs and elsewhere, was to get these Jews to play sports. In New York City, even Talmud Torah, old-world centers of learning, started providing gyms. The Ys were originally closed on Saturdays in observance of the Sabbath, but soon began offering exercise classes on Saturdays, an acknowledgment of the secular realities of life in America. Of the more than twenty thousand YMHA members, few were observant. But they were still Jews. Turn-of-the-century reports from the 92nd Street Y show that its only facility that was more used than those for sports was its reading room.

For children of Jewish immigrants, Americanization meant sports, baseball and boxing being by far the most popular. Not so for their immigrant parents. There are endless Yiddish jokes about children embarrassed by unassimilated parents.

> A father wanted to attend a reception with his son. "Please, Dad," the son pleaded. "Don't be embarrassing. Try to act normal."
>
> "I'll be completely assimilated," the father promised, and at the reception the son was pleased to see his father at the bar ordering a martini, a good American assimilated drink.
>
> "Dry?" asked the bartender.
>
> "*Neyn, a dank. Tsvey ist genug*," the father replied while the son cringed. No, thank you. Two would be fine. (The Yiddish word for three is pronounced "dry.")

There were two conflicting views of sports. Greenberg was of the school that wanted to leave the shtetl behind and become as American as quickly as possible. Baseball was one way of doing that. But there was a second approach, famously articulated by the philosopher Horace Meyer Kallen, who coined the phrase "cultural pluralism." He believed that the strength of America was that each immigrant group could assimilate while keeping something of its old culture, thereby enriching the fabric of American life. Many of Greenberg's fans, unlike the ballplayer himself, were of this second school that not only wanted to see a Jew play baseball, but also wanted him to be distinctly Jewish as a player.

In *The Celebrant*, a 1983 novel by Eric Rolfe Greenberg—no relation to Hank, even though some passages read like the ballplayer's autobiography—the seventeen-year-old narrator confronts his parents with his plan to become a professional baseball player. He struggles to convince them that he could earn a living playing baseball, but even then, "though my parents came to believe that I'd actually be paid to play ball the issue went far deeper than money. We had not crossed the ocean to find disgraceful employment."

That was the problem—professional sports provided disgraceful employment. Irving Howe quotes the singer-comedian Eddie Cantor, born Isador Iskowitz on the Lower East Side in 1892, recalling that the worst thing his grandmother could say to him when she got angry was, "You—you—you baseball player, you!" But in 2004, in an article on the late immigrant pitcher Izzy Goldstein, a *Jewish Daily* reporter wrote, "For young Jews, however, baseball is more than statistics. Playing ball has been a conduit for blending into the American mainstream."

Assimilation, including the arguments for and against it, is one of the great themes of Jewish history. Jewish scholars like to draw a distinction between assimilation, being completely absorbed into the non-Jewish world, and acculturation, adopting non-Jewish culture. The enduring questions—How Jewish should a Jew be? How different should a Jew be? Is it necessary to maintain differentness to preserve Jewishness, or is differentness just something that is imposed by anti-Semites? Is playing sports acting like a Gentile? Does a player's Jewishness make him a different kind of athlete, and does his athleticism make him a different kind of Jew?—challenged and continue to challenge. Hank Greenberg had to find answers to all of these questions in his pioneering career. As impressive as his statistics is that he did so with so much grace.

2

A Beautiful Swing

> Humboldt could hit like a sonofabitch on
> the sandlot. With his shoulders, just imagine
> how much beef there went into his swing.
> —Saul Bellow, *Humboldt's Gift*

> Surely it would have put me on a somewhat
> different footing with this game that I loved with
> all my heart, not simply for the fun of playing it
> (fun was secondary, really), but for the mythic and
> aesthetic dimension that it gave to an American
> boy's life—particularly to one whose grand-
> parents could hardly speak English.
> —Philip Roth, "My Baseball Years"

AMONG THE historic two million–strong wave of Jews who left eastern Europe for America was David Greenberg from the Moldavian town of Roman, in Romania.

In New York, Greenberg met Sarah Schwartz, who had immigrated from Falticena in a neighboring province of Romania. David and Sarah met at a *landsmanshaft*, a social club for Jewish immigrants from the same area or district. There were thousands of such *landsmanshaftn* in the beginning of the twentieth century, many of them, like the one where the Greenbergs met, on Manhattan's Lower East Side. Today the word *landsman* is used by Jews to denote a fellow Jew, but a century ago it referred to Jews from the same town or region.

David and Sarah married and settled into an apartment on Barrow Street in Greenwich Village. They had their first child, Ben, in 1907, then a daughter Lillian, and then in 1911, "forty-five minutes after the New Year," as Hank liked to say about his birthday, their son Hyman was born. About a year later they moved to a sixth-floor walk-up on nearby Perry Street, into a building whose tenants were mostly Yiddish-speaking immigrants. Hank remembered it as a tough neighborhood. "Kids down in the Village thought the national pastime was beating up kids of other nationalities." The Irish beat up the Italians and the Italians beat up the Irish, and on Halloween they both went after the Jews. It was a tradition among Catholic kids in the neighborhood, and Jewish children knew to stay home from school on Halloween to avoid being attacked. In the last years of his life Hank Greenberg started recording his remembrances for an autobiography he never completed. In the volume edited by the sportswriter Ira Berkow, Greenberg recalled how non-Jewish kids would put rocks in a sock to hit Jewish kids on the head on Halloween. He remembered his mother warning him if he went out on Halloween, "Look out, don't get the sock."

He also remembered, "There was no place to play baseball, nobody thought about the game or missed it."

The neighborhoods of lower Manhattan were so crowded and densely populated that there was no space for a baseball field. Jewish social reformers of the time were arguing for the construction of public parks in urban slums so that the children of immigrants could "get some fresh air" and play sports, which would teach them to be true Americans. Among the Jewish advocates of such parks were the labor leader Samuel Gompers and the public health advocate Lillian Ward. But many of the slum residents opposed this initiative because they regarded parks as a waste of valuable space needed to relieve the desperate housing shortage. The parks that did get built were used for neighborhood baseball games, but they were also the scenes of frequent violence as one ethnic group fought to take over the park and exclude the others.

The athletic Jews in crowded lower Manhattan became either basketball players or boxers. Basketball was invented by James Naismith, a Canadian, in 1891, at the height of Jewish immigration. Because it was an ideal urban sport, Jews dominated it for decades. Women's basketball was invented by a Jew, Lithuanian-born Senda Berenson, sister of the famous art critic Bernard Berenson, and was also a popular Jewish sport.

The Jewish Ys, settlement houses, and other centers for immigrants offered basketball and started producing talented players. When Jewish high school teams toured, they introduced the game to non-Jewish communities. But from the first, they were in conflict with Jewish law, since they found that their best chance of drawing a large crowd was to play on Friday nights.

Most of the new Jewish boxers in the early twentieth century were American-born products of New York slums, and their immigrant parents typically were extremely unhappy about their son's career choice. Though the profession was new to their culture, the idea of the Jewish tough guy who could beat up the *goyim* was not. Back in the shtetls there would be a few particularly tough young men who knew how to use their fists to protect the community from anti-Semites. The *ba'al guf*, or tough guy, was an admired character in Yiddish literature, the subject and title of the Ukrainian-born poet Haim Nachman Bialik's first short story in 1899.

In American slums Jewish kids learned to be that character and take on the Irish or other ethnics from adjacent slums. The boxer Louis Wallach grew up in an Orthodox home on the Lower East Side and learned to fight by facing the Irish when he had to walk from Second to Third Avenue on his way to school. Wallach earned a dental degree from New York University but still pursued a lightweight fight career under the name Leach Cross. In 1906 he won his first professional fight in two rounds, but he did not tell his parents because the event had taken place on a Friday night. He explained the bruise on his face as an accident he had suffered while playing basketball with friends.

For his first twenty-six professional bouts he would come home afterward and tell his parents that he had been working late on a "dental project." According to the Jewish sports historian Ken Blady, on December 20, 1911, Cross fought K. O. Brown to a ten-round no-decision, during which he loosened most of Brown's front teeth. The next day Brown's manager took him to see a dentist, Dr. Louis Wallach.

Many Jewish fighters changed their names, sometimes to avoid anti-Semitism, but often to hide their career from their parents. In 1914 the middleweight title was won by Al McCoy, originally Harry Rudolph, the son of a kosher butcher in Brownsville. For a while Irish names were fashionable for Jews and other non-Irish fighters simply because the Irish had a reputation for being the best fighters. A sign that Jews had established themselves in the sport was that by the 1920s, some of the new Italian fighters took Jewish names, including Sammy Mandella, who fought as Sammy Mandell. There were also Jewish fighters who changed their not particularly Jewish names to seem more Jewish. The 1923 junior lightweight champion Jack Bernstein had changed his name from Jack Dudick.

By the time Hank Greenberg dreamed of becoming a ballplayer, the idea that Jews could excel as boxers was well accepted, with such well-known names as featherweight champion Abe "the little Hebrew" Attell, Benny Leonard, lightweight champion Al Singer, light heavyweight champion Slapsie Maxie Rosenbloom, and flyweight champion Johnny Rosner. The idea of Jewish athletes was no longer new.

In 1916, when Hank was five years old, the Greenbergs had their fourth child, Joe. The following year, they moved to the Bronx. According to Hank, they moved because the neighborhood was getting too crowded and tough and the Jews were moving out.

The Greenbergs settled in Crotona Park, which, though now part of the South Bronx, was then a handsome green and wooded stretch of land. The nearby Grand Concourse, where Jews would soon move into luxury apartment buildings on a wide boulevard, was still farmland. Crotona Park started to develop late in the nineteenth century as trolley service was instituted to connect the area to the Third Avenue elevated train. In 1904, just before the Greenbergs arrived, the neighborhood got subway service. So David Greenberg could live by a park in the country and commute every day to his textile sponging business in lower Manhattan, where wool was finished to make it feel softer and less scratchy. Crotona Park was one of several prime areas in the Bronx where Jewish immigrants who were starting to do a little better moved to get away from tenement life. The shaded avenue on one side, Crotona Park East, was sometimes referred to as the Central Park West of the Bronx. Fine brick exteriors with ornate masonry, marble lobbies, even elevators were features of the neighborhood buildings.

It is not clear how affluent the Greenbergs were, and later press accounts that said Hank Greenberg came from a wealthy family have been attacked as anti-Semitic. Yet Julius Wolk, who was born six months before Hank and lived a block away, said, "The Greenbergs were the richest people in the neighborhood. Most people were workers. Greenberg had become wealthy in garments, sponging cloth. He built his own house on the park, Crotona Park North, a beautiful brick house."

Jewish immigrants of David Greenberg's generation had started with virtually nothing, so if they managed to own a little garment business they were seen in the community as successes, even wealthy, though by other standards they were simply middle class. Wolk recalled that the Greenbergs owned another building similar to the one he lived in—three floors with a seven-room apartment on each floor. They rented out the three apartments in this building on the corner of Crotona Park and Crotona Avenue, which Wolk remembered clearly because his future in-laws were among the tenants.

There were a few Italian families in the neighborhood, and Wolk remembered a Polish family, but the overwhelming majority of the population was Jewish. This too was part of the appeal of Crotona Park. There were no worries about going out on Halloween. Most of the neighborhood's Jews of Hank Greenberg's generation, when asked about their childhood brushes with anti-Semitism, responded the way Wolk did: "Anti-Semitism? I grew up in the Bronx."

Most Jews in the neighborhood were observant, keeping kosher homes, shopping in the Jewish stores along tree-lined Crotona Avenue and Tremont Avenue, buying their kosher groceries from Shapiro's and their meat from Ackner's, the kosher butcher. Hank and everyone else said that the Greenbergs were Orthodox. But it was the Orthodoxy of their hardworking immigrant generation, different from the Orthodoxy of today. David and Sarah dispensed with head coverings, hats and wigs, for street and house wear. David's face was clean-shaven. But they did go regularly to synagogue, observe the holidays, and keep kosher, like almost everyone else in the neighborhood. Reform and Conservative Judaism, which had begun to spread in nineteenth-century America, had not taken root with twentieth-century eastern European immigrants like the Greenbergs. Either you were Orthodox or you were non-practicing.

This casual version of Orthodoxy was the religion Hank grew up in. His father went to work and his mother maintained a Jewish home, cleaning the house out for Passover and baking a challah every Friday for Sabbath dinner. When he was thirteen, Hank was bar mitzvahed. Not studious in general, he particularly disliked learning Hebrew. Many years later he told the American Jewish Committee, "I didn't know what I was reading. It meant nothing to me." When he was older he joked about the traditional gift of a gold watch for bar mitzvah. But he kept the gold watch that his aunt gave him his entire life.

Greenberg seemed destined to be an athlete, but had the Greenbergs remained in crowded lower Manhattan he probably would have become a boxer or basketball player. Transplanted to leafy Crotona Park, though, Greenberg wanted only to play baseball. Wolk remembered, "Living near the park was beautiful. There was a great deal of socializing and boys and girls would meet in the park. It was filled with all kinds of vegetation. You could rent a boat and paddle on Indian Lake, in the winter you rented ice skates and everyone skated on the lake. There were two baseball diamonds. We all lived on the baseball field, and Hank would get us to pitch to him for hours." The park also had courts for tennis and handball, sports that became Hank Greenberg's lifelong obsession, far outlasting his interest in baseball.

Hank, unlike Babe Ruth and some of the other greats of baseball, was not considered "a natural talent," an assessment that he frequently acknowledged and that was echoed by his school coaches and ultimately his colleagues in major league baseball. Instead, Greenberg felt his success demonstrated what could be accomplished by hard work and determination. "If you practice the way I did," he said, "all day long, day after day—you're bound to get pretty good."

He was not particularly graceful and felt self-conscious about his size. A head taller than anyone else at school, he called himself "a freak." All his life he had a way of ducking his head as if to appear less tall than he was. This quirk was evident as he loped around the bases after hitting a home run, bobbing like a giraffe trotting through a tunnel. On his 1932 application for membership in the 92nd Street Y, he reported a height of six feet, three and a quarter inches—three quarters of an inch shy of his actual height. It is not clear whether he was intentionally playing down his height or had just measured shorter because he was stooping. The following year, his first full season in the major leagues, he checked in at the Y a little more successful and one quarter inch taller. But the Tigers listed him at six foot four.

He had size and power. In 1937 he posed for a photo of the top players of the American League All-Star team. The seven of them—Lou Gehrig, Joe Cronin, Bill Dickey, Joe DiMaggio, Charlie Gehringer, Jimmie Foxx, and Hank Greenberg—lined up in uniform, each holding a bat. Tigers, Yankees, and Red Sox—they were all future Hall of Famers, seven of the all-time biggest names in baseball. The one on the end, Hank Greenberg, looks like someone Photoshopped him in. He is on a completely different scale from the others, a full head taller. Next to Greenberg, Jimmie Foxx, a muscular six-foot-tall power hitter, looks like a stocky little man, the letters RED SOX on his chest barely above Greenberg's waist.

But young Hymie Greenberg, as he was known, though gangly and awkward, believed that if he practiced hard enough he could harness the power in his body to create a perfect swing. And so he spent every moment of daylight he could steal away from school to realize this physical act of power and beauty.

"Hank was the tallest among us and the best athlete," Julius Wolk recalled. "He was deeply immersed in playing baseball. He literally spent all his time on the ball field in Crotona Park. He would have one of us pitch to him as he stood at home plate. He would just clobber the ball. We knew he was going to be good."

Lester Pashkin, who grew up a short walk from Crotona Park, said, "We all played baseball in the neighborhood. That's what we did." Pashkin and other kids from the neighborhood used to hike about thirty blocks to Yankee Stadium, where the Yankees would use them as bat boys and ball boys whose job it was to retrieve foul balls. Their only pay was a scuffed up, grass-stained baseball, which they would either sell for a dollar or take back to Crotona Park. Real major league baseballs were scarce in those days.

Hank said that what allowance he had was spent on tape for balls. He hit the ball so hard that the leather cover would soon tear off. He and his cronies would tape it so it would last a while longer, but after a time that cover would get torn off too. The string around the rubber center would start unraveling, so they would tape it up again until Hank walloped it a few more times and it got too small and finally had to be replaced.

He tried to find volunteers to pitch to him or chase down the fly balls, but sometimes, when he couldn't find a friend, he would pay a small amount for the service. He usually had a few quarters to spend because in that neighborhood kids would play baseball for quarters. Each player would put up a quarter, and the winning team would split the pot. Hank generally made sure that his team won. Winning was already very important to him.

Years later, when Hank became a star, it seemed to him that a lot more people were claiming to have pitched to him on the ball field in Crotona Park than could possibly have done so. He said that men twenty years younger would come up to him and say, "I used to shag balls for you in the Bronx." Today, the few nonagenarians left from the old neighborhood laugh at how many people insisted that a relative of the ballplayer lived in their building when they were growing up—seemingly half of Crotona Park. If you were Jewish and from the Bronx, you wanted a connection with Hank Greenberg.

In accounts of Greenberg's approach to practice, the word *scientific* is often used. In his 1980 interview with the American Jewish Committee he described the way he worked as "just like a scientist would be devoted to medicine."

In reality his approach was like that of his father, who put in long hours to prosper in the garment trade, and his mother, who labored around the clock, cleaning their ten-room house, looking after four children, doing her own baking. David and Sarah passed on their immigrant work ethic to their children. The other three applied it more conventionally—studying hard, going to college, succeeding in business. But Hank applied that same ethic to swinging a bat.

At the root of the Hank Greenberg mystique, why this Jewish baseball player more than any other became a Jewish icon, was an unconscious ability to rewrite the Jewish stereotype. He threw out the negative stereotypes and kept the positive ones. He was big and strong like Jews weren't supposed to be, but his Jewishness was unmistakably in his face. But even a big, strong Jewish star athlete was not going to behave like a non-Jewish star athlete. He was not going to drink and chase women and get out of shape like a Babe Ruth. Hank Greenberg the Jewish athlete studied his game and worked at it with great discipline. Asked what they admired about Greenberg, his fans often mentioned how hardworking he was.

All his life he laughed at being looked down upon for playing baseball. "Jewish women on my block . . . would point me out as a good-for-nothing, a loafer, and a bum who always wanted to play baseball rather than go to school," Greenberg recalled to the *Detroit Jewish Chronicle* in 1935. "Friends and relatives sympathized with my mother because she was the parent of a big gawk who cared more for baseball than schoolbooks. I was Mrs. Greenberg's disgrace," he said with characteristic self-effacement.

"'Mrs. Greenberg has such nice children,'" he claimed they would say. "'Too bad one of them has to be a bum.'" *Bum* was a word commonly used by Jews to describe kids who spent too much time on baseball. He remembered his mother calling baseball "a bum's game." The *Forward*'s popular section of letters, the famous *Bintel Brief*, or letter bundle, was filled with denunciations of the game. "What is the point of a crazy game like baseball?" one reader protested. "I want my boy to grow up to be a mentsch, not a wild American runner." But by the time of Greenberg's childhood, baseball had gained a measure of acceptance in the Jewish world. The *Forward* had moved from criticizing baseball to trying to explain it to greenhorns. In fact, for an immigrant people struggling to be American, baseball had taken on considerable importance. Solomon Schechter, one of the leading Conservative rabbis in America, is frequently quoted as having said, "Unless you can play baseball, you will never get to be a rabbi in America." Opposition to baseball was becoming an old-fashioned attitude, but there were still a lot of old-fashioned people in Crotona Park.

Hank had a number of run-ins with his father over staying out too long playing ball. Without bitterness, Greenberg recalled his father occasionally hitting him with "a strap." But Wolk remembers, "His father was very enthusiastic about his playing . . . his most ardent fan. He would sit in the grandstand watching Hank perform and cheer him with great enthusiasm."

Contrary to the intellectual curiosity he displayed as a mature adult, as a boy Hank showed little interest in schoolwork, neglecting his homework if it cut into practice time. At school he played baseball as well as basketball and worked on both for long hours after school. By his own reckoning, he spent 85 percent of his time on sports and 15 on his studies, which was all he needed to get passing grades. He did not even take time off to date girls.

Later in life, he found it difficult to explain this lack of intellectual life and complete obsession with sports. At one point he mused that he might have been drawn to sports as a way of hiding. He remembered being laughed at in school due to his unusual height. "How's the air up there?" was one of the taunts that stayed with him all his life.

So he lost himself in sports, an activity in which he would become famous for ignoring taunts. And when he was a boy, the batter's box and the basketball court were places where no one laughed at his size. All his life he believed that his physical abilities would never let him down, so long as he worked as hard as he possibly could.

This was the way Greenberg made himself into a ballplayer. Though he was a mediocre defensive first baseman, he would learn a move and practice it over and over again until he could automatically turn the play well. And there could never be enough batting practice to satisfy him. In later years teammates and opponents alike acknowledged him as the hardest working player they had ever seen.

One of the reasons baseball fans so love the sport is that it involves certain physical acts of remarkable beauty. One of the most beautiful sights in the history of baseball was Hank Greenberg's swing. The calmly poised body seemed to have some special set of springs with a trigger that released each powerful muscle one at a time as the bat sliced through the air, propeller-like, with such clean speed and power that it was hard to believe it was a man-made motion.

Hank Greenberg did not think in terms of career; he played to win. In fact, he said that he was barely aware of major league baseball until he went to high school. Both Yankee Stadium and the Polo Grounds, where the Giants played, were within walking distance of Crotona Park—long walks, true, but people in the Bronx were used to walking. Even Hank's high school was more than an hour's walk away.

It was an exciting era in New York baseball. With the Dodgers, Giants, and Yankees, New York had at least one team in the World Series eight out of ten years in the 1920s. Three of those series took place entirely in the neighborhood—with the Giants versus the Yankees. As a kid, Hank, the future American League star, was a National League fan, rooting for the Giants, who played across the Harlem River in Manhattan. The Giants were the established stars, but the Yankees, with Babe Ruth and Lou Gehrig and a brand new stadium, were the newcomers on the rise.

Giant scores were posted in shop windows in the Bronx, and people gathered in front of the windows to follow the World Series. Even though baseball tickets cost just fifty cents, going to a ballpark was a rare luxury. In 1925, when Hank was fourteen years old, his father took him to the Polo Grounds to watch his first major league game. The Giants beat the Phillies in a doubleheader. Decades later Greenberg still talked about the seven hits by second baseman Frankie Frisch, a Bronx native and the team captain.

In the 1920s, and for decades after, baseball was the only professional team sport of any significance in America. Greenberg recalled in his autobiography, "In my childhood, baseball was everything, the only sport that really mattered, and a star baseball player was a hero on par with Sergeant York or Charles Lindbergh." Who wouldn't want to be that star?

Still, when he attended James Monroe High School in the Bronx, Hank was not yet dreaming of the major leagues, about which he knew little. He went out for every sport he could in high school—baseball, soccer, basketball, football, and track, lettering in all except track. In soccer and basketball, he led his team to city championships. But the baseball team was eliminated in the finals, even though the school had recruited twenty-year-old Izzy Goldstein, a semipro who later went on to play for the Detroit Tigers, to pose as a student and pitch for the team. At the time, Hank's favorite sport, and his best one, was basketball, for which he also spent endless hours practicing. After all, he was a head taller than everyone he played with.

His basketball coach, Irwin Dickstein, said, "Hank never played the games, he worked them. He wasn't a natural athlete, his reactions were slow and he had trouble coordinating his big body. He couldn't run a lick because he had flat feet, but even in high school he was practicing quick starts to overcome that handicap." His parents thought professional sport was a foolish dream, but in fact their son was more of a pragmatist than a dreamer. "Basketball was not a sport you could pursue," he would later explain. The only team sport that afforded an athlete a chance to earn a good living in the 1920s was baseball, and that was why Hank chose to become a baseball player instead of pursuing basketball.

Like his immigrant parents and his siblings, Hank was looking for a path to a better life. What set him apart from the other members of his family was that he envisioned a life that was more glamorous and worldly. As for many kids from the outer boroughs, the wonders of Manhattan loomed large in his dreams. He wanted to go to Manhattan to eat and shop and do the things they did down there. Looking back in his autobiography he pointed out that even when the World Series took place in the Bronx, people in the Bronx didn't go. The seats went to Manhattan people. He did not crave wealth, but he understood that money was, as it had been for his parents, a key to opening the door to a better life.

Yet sports were his passion and his mission. His plan was to do well in high school sports so that he could get onto a college baseball team. His parents, meanwhile, hoped that he would do well in high school, go to college, and become a doctor. As Hank's son, Steve, put it, "Doctor, lawyer, come into the family business, a textile business, [any of] that would have been fine. One uncle was a jeweler. That was all fine. Schoolteacher would have been fine too but the point was, Jewish kids didn't drop out of college and go play baseball with the goyim." Steve Greenberg saw a rebellious side to his father, the son of immigrants who was determined to go his own way. "My dad sort of reacted against that a little bit, being an immigrant's son," said Steve. "He wanted to be as American as possible when he was a kid, which led to baseball." Irving Howe wrote of the younger generation in *World of Our Fathers*, "What they were struggling for was nothing less than the persuasion that they had as much right as anyone else to feel at home on this earth, and what their parents were saying was no, Jews could not feel at home on this earth."

By the mid-1920s Hank Greenberg's beloved Giants were no longer the star team. The Polo Grounds, where he had seen his first game, was the fourth field used by the Giants, all of them in upper Manhattan and all called the Polo Grounds because the original one, near Central Park, really had been used for polo. With two tiers of grandstands and a capacity of 34,000, the final Polo Grounds was the largest ballpark in baseball at the time. It had a very deep center field but offered short home run targets in left and right field, and the park was generally considered to favor hitters.

In 1913 the Giants rented the Polo Grounds to the Yankees, and the two competitors shared the park, which worked well when the American League Yankees were on the bottom and the National League Giants on the top. But Babe Ruth joined the Yankees in 1920 and started hitting home runs in record numbers over those short walls. As a result, attendance at Yankee games doubled, making them for the first time a bigger draw than the Giants, who had up to then been baseball's most popular team. In 1922 the Giants told their tenants to leave, and the Yankees moved less than a mile away, building the first three-deck baseball park, the first to be called a stadium, and began to fill it with crowds eager to see the powerful and flamboyant Ruth.

To compete, the Giants expanded seating capacity at the Polo Grounds to 54,555. But they were not filling the stands, even though they were playing well and winning pennants. Thinking of ways he might help his financially struggling team, Giant manager John J. McGraw had an idea. He thought that if the Giants had a great Jewish player, the large Jewish population of New York City would flock to the Polo Grounds. The Yankees at the time were trying to draw Italians with Tony Lazzeri, a big-hitting second baseman from San Francisco. America was a nation of immigrants, and most ballclubs were using the ethnic mix of their rosters to draw fans.

The growth of anti-Semitism in America can be traced in the names of Jewish players. While earlier Jewish players used their real names, many of the players of Greenberg's youth changed their names to avoid the increasingly virulent anti-Semitism in baseball organizations, among fans, and in the press. Arthur Cohen, born in San Francisco, played seven seasons, mostly for the Cincinnati Reds, as infielder Sam Bohne. In 1915 Bostonian Henry Lipschitz played two games at third base for the Philadelphia Athletics as Henry Bostick, and four years later, Michael Myron Silverman of Cleveland appeared as shortstop Jesse Baker in one game for the Washington Senators. Philip Cohen, from Paterson, New Jersey, played a game at third base in 1905 for the Highlanders (before they became the Yankees) as Phil Cooney. Ed Cohen pitched two innings for his hometown Chicago White Sox under the name Ed Corey in 1918. As we've seen, the Ukrainian-born Reuben Cohen played as Reuben Ewing. Harry Cohen from Hamburg,

Arkansas, who pitched for three teams in four seasons in the decade before Greenberg was born, used the name Harry Kane. Cohen would have been one of the most common names in baseball but for name changes inspired by anti-Semitism.

But New Yorkers were different. They were used to being around other Jews. Kids who grew up near Crotona Park did not have a lot of experience with anti-Semitism because they grew up in a Jewish world—one of the reasons the Greenbergs had moved there. If there was the occasional anti-Semite, there were a lot more Jews. As Greenberg said in his autobiography, "If you lived in a Jewish neighborhood and everybody was Jewish, all you knew was that there were goyim—the Gentiles—out in the world, but you didn't know about anti-Semitism."

The New York players seldom changed their names. Bob Berman was a New York–born catcher for the Senators for two games in 1918. Jake Pitler, also from New York, was the Pittsburgh Pirates' regular second baseman in 1917. Al Schacht, another native New Yorker who signed with the Washington Senators in 1919, once wrote, "There is talk that I am Jewish—just because my father was Jewish, my mother is Jewish, I speak Yiddish and once studied to be a rabbi and a cantor. Well, that's how rumors get started."

Moe Berg was born a few blocks from the Polo Grounds in upper Manhattan to Jewish immigrant parents. His father, a pharmacist, expected his children to become doctors. Moe's brother Sam, a doctor, said of Moe's desire to play baseball, "He was a genetic deviant." Berg was the rare baseball Ivy Leaguer, playing shortstop for Princeton while studying philosophy and Romance languages. He graduated magna cum laude in modern languages. Then he signed with the Brooklyn Dodgers immediately after graduation, over the strong objections of his father, who regarded baseball as a waste of time and, unlike Greenberg's critical father, never celebrated his son's accomplishments, refusing ever to see him.

Berg was shuffled around to various teams and ended up a catcher for the Boston Red Sox. In the off-season he had time for his intellectual pursuits, including one year studying experimental phonetics at the Sorbonne in Paris, and another winter he entered Columbia Law School. He was admitted to the New York Bar in 1929. In 1939, on the rare occasion of Berg's hitting a home run—one of only six in his career—a columnist quipped that he should celebrate by learning another language. "He can speak a dozen languages," it was repeatedly said about Berg, "but he can't hit in any of them." Equally famous was the assessment of his playing by scout Mike Gonzalez: "Good field, no hit."

McGraw got his Jewish player at the end of the 1923 season. Starting with his Hebraic name, Mose Solomon seemed an ideal Jewish star for the Giants because he was a big-hitting native New Yorker. He was also a bit of a ba'al guf, a Jewish tough guy, with a reputation for beating up people who made anti-Semitic comments. Nicknamed "the Rabbi of Swat," in 1923 he batted .421 with 40 doubles, 15 triples, and 49 home runs for the Hutchinson Wheat Shockers in the Class C. At the end of the season McGraw brought him up to the Giants, where he hit .375 in 8 at-bats. But Solomon was a reverse Moe Berg— good hit, no field. Today he might have been a designated hitter, but in 1923 there was no place for a player who couldn't catch and throw balls and made constant errors. After his two-game stay with the Giants, he was returned to the minors.

The Giants signed their next would-be Jewish star, Andy Cohen, in 1926, and for a time it seemed he was on his way to becoming a Jewish baseball legend. He played second base, shortstop, and third base with remarkable defensive skills. The press noted that he looked Jewish; in the words of the *Sporting News*, he had "all the natural characteristics (physically) of his race—thick, dark hair, dark skin and keen mentality."

There was a rush to write about the new Jewish player—about his birth to immigrants in Baltimore, his move to Texas at an early age, and his refusal to insult his parents by changing his given name, Andrew Howard Cohen. In 1928 the *New York Times* ran an article with the headline, "Andy Cohen Keeps His Name." Unfortunately, throughout the article the reporter got that name wrong, improbably calling the player Andrew Jackson Cohen. "He had done pretty well up to then as Andrew Jackson Cohen and he would continue under that name," read the *Times* story. The press never forgot his Jewishness, though, always referring to him with phrases such as "the young Jewish boy." And there were numerous "Cohen at the Bat" riffs in the papers on the famous Ernest Thayer poem. A proud Jew made good copy, and Cohen played well and stood up to hecklers who shouted anti-Semitic epithets at him. This was what McGraw had in mind when he brought Cohen up from the Texas League.

McGraw wanted to keep him, but could use him only to fill in because he had regular players at all the infield positions. Cohen, in search of an everyday starting position, left the Giants at the end of the year for the Buffalo Bisons in the International League. There, in 1927, he was a star and a cherished hero to the Buffalo Jewish community, all of which made McGraw want him back. At the end of 1927 he traded the future Hall of Fame second baseman Rogers Hornsby to the Boston Braves, opening a position for Cohen.

Billed as "the great Jewish hope," Cohen returned to the Polo Grounds with huge expectations from the fans and the management. He was to be the Jewish Rogers Hornsby. On opening day 1928, the Giants played the Braves. Cohen was the star player in a 5–3 victory, responsible for four out of five of the Giants runs, hitting two singles and a double, knocking in two runs, and scoring two. After the game the crowd rushed onto the field, where fans lifted Cohen to their shoulders. But his fielding was disappointing, and after two seasons McGraw sent him to the Newark Bears to perfect his defensive skills. In 1930 Cohen played brilliant defense but then broke his leg. Sadly, he never got back into the majors, and some historians have speculated that he was under too much pressure to be a Jewish star. Eventually he became a vaudeville star, appearing on the circuit with an Irish teammate, Shanty Hogan. Theirs was a popular routine billed as Cohen and Hogan, or in Boston, as Hogan and Cohen.

Before Hank Greenberg, Andy Cohen was as close as baseball had ever come to having a Jewish superstar. There is no record of the extent to which Greenberg was following the trajectory of Cohen's career in the press. But as a Jew from the Bronx playing for the Giants, Cohen almost certainly caught Hank's interest.

That the Yankees were able to rise from one of the worst teams in the American League to one of the best in a few years in the 1920s is partly due to a not particularly successful major leaguer named Paul Krichell. Krichell had played for two seasons as a backup catcher for the St. Louis Browns in 1911–12. He then coached for the Red Sox. In 1920 he was hired by the Yankees as a scout and signed, among many others, Bill Dickey, Lou Gehrig, and Tony Lazzeri. In 1928 he became interested in a pitcher at nearby James Monroe High School and went to see him in a game. The pitcher turned out to be disappointing, but the huge first baseman with the beautiful swing was someone to watch.

Greenberg graduated the following year and in accordance with the wishes of his parents, who were determined to put all of their children through college, he enrolled at New York University with an athletic scholarship for basketball. But he was already earning more money than most professional basketball players did as a semiprofessional baseball player for the

Red Bank Towners. Just as in high school, he spent much more of his college time playing sports than studying.

John McGraw, in his quest for a Jewish player for the Giants, had already looked at Greenberg and was not interested, which might have been a blow to a Giant fan from the Bronx. Greenberg never complained about it, though, perhaps because there were other teams interested. He continued to play baseball in Crotona Park, in New Jersey, and anywhere else he had an opportunity. And wherever he played, there was Paul Krichell on the sidelines, taking notes.

Greenberg got his first press coverage when he started playing for a semipro team in Brooklyn in 1929. A *New York Times* sportswriter was impressed by "Hyman Greenberg, youthful first baseman for the Parkways . . . " Soon a scout for Detroit got interested in Greenberg and tried to steal him out from under Krichell and the Yankees by giving him a position on a Massachusetts team. With an important competitor interested, Krichell decided that it was time for the Yankees to make their move. But the Yankees' bargaining power was not ideal: Lou Gehrig, their first baseman, was the most durable player in baseball, en route to 2,130 consecutive games played. As a backup for Lou Gehrig, Greenberg would never play.

Krichell took Hank to a game in Yankee Stadium, and they sat together in a front-row box behind the Yankee dugout. Krichell tried to convince Greenberg that Gehrig's career was almost over, pointing out that his batting average had declined. "He's all washed up," Krichell whispered. But with Gehrig standing only a few feet away, Hank was awestruck. Sixty years later in his autobiography he still sounded that way: "His shoulders were a yard wide and his legs looked like mighty oak trees. I'd never seen such sheer brute strength." Hank vowed not to play for the Yankees behind Gehrig. Nor did he want to play in Yankee Stadium, which having been built for Ruth, was designed to be an easy place for lefties to hit home runs over the right field wall. But it was hard on right-handed batters like Greenberg, who pulled the ball toward the left field fence, which in Yankee Stadium was far away.

Meanwhile, the Senators and the Tigers both made offers. As Greenberg recalled it in his autobiography, when he told his father that the Tigers were offering him $9,000, David Greenberg whistled and repeated, "Nine thousand dollars. You mean they want to give you that kind of money to go out and play with the baseball?" But his father wanted to know above all if Hank could finish college. Greenberg had made an arrangement with the Tigers that if he signed with them they would wait four years until he graduated from N.Y.U. Once he was reassured that his son would finish college, David Greenberg advised Hank to "take the money," saying, "I thought baseball was a game. But it's a business—apparently a very good business." If it was a business, it was a legitimate activity for his son.

Because baseball was indeed a business in 1929, when the Yankees heard Greenberg was signing with Detroit for $9,000 they immediately offered him $10,000. But Greenberg turned the Yankees down, mainly because of his misgivings about the Gehrig situation. George McQuinn, a first baseman one year Greenberg's senior, did sign with the Yankees and spent his potentially best years, in his twenties, in their farm system waiting for Gehrig's retirement; finally McQuinn was traded at the age of twenty-six. Considering that Greenberg played most of his greatest seasons when he was in his twenties, had he signed with the Yankees he might have ended up no more famous than George McQuinn.

Greenberg was smart, not only about how he played baseball, but about how he managed his career. In those days, there were no agents, and players did all of their own negotiating. The Yankee ownership became furious when Joe DiMaggio tried to have a fight manager negotiate for him. He was told that this was just not done in baseball. Greenberg was one of the few players who was a good negotiator on his own behalf. During the Depression, when salaries, even Babe Ruth's, were being cut every year, Greenberg consistently made lucrative deals. He believed, as his father had, that the legitimacy of a baseball career derived from the fact that it was a business, and he ran his career that way.

The only thing Greenberg was not particularly smart about was studying. He spent his freshman year at N.Y.U., but once spring arrived and the baseball season was getting under way, he knew that he could not wait three more years to begin his career. He told the Tigers he wanted to start that season. His parents remained supportive, but he felt their disappointment. His three siblings all earned college degrees. Throughout his life he never missed an opportunity to point out that he was the family "disgrace" who never finished college. As if on a lifelong program to educate himself, he read book after book, always nonfiction. The people close to Greenberg toward the end of his life describe him as an essentially happy man with little anxiety or self-doubt, but he did make frequent reference to his lack of higher education. If it had really bothered him, he could have gone back to school, but what seemed to upset him the most was that he had disappointed his parents. Clearly, he cared a great deal about their opinion of him.

They were proud of him with or without a degree. But this was not the way it was supposed to happen for Jewish kids from rising immigrant families. They were supposed to be like Saul Bellow's Humboldt, who forgot all about playing baseball once he started going to the library. Or, as it was put by writer Philip Roth, who grew up in New Jersey, "Playing baseball was not what the Jewish boys of our lower-middle-class neighborhood were expected to do in later life for a living."

At the turn of the century, when outraged immigrant parents were denouncing baseball in letters to the Yiddish *Jewish Daily Forward*, Abraham Cahan, the paper's co-founder and editor, answered with an editorial in which he argued that Jewish boys should be allowed to play baseball—especially since no one could stop them—with one important caveat: as long as it did not interfere with their education. At the time Jews made up 3.6 percent of the American population but 9 percent of all college students. In New York City almost half the college students were Jewish.

At the end of February 1930, Hank left New York on a train for spring training in Florida, a young man off to what his son Steve described as "this alien world otherwise known as Gentile America." He knew little about Florida and almost nothing about Detroit.

But if it was an alien world, it was one he gladly entered. Years later, when asked why he went into baseball, he had a one-word answer: "Escape." Eli Wohlgelernter, interviewing Greenberg for the American Jewish Committee, asked him what he was trying to escape from. Hank said, "From being in the Bronx and being in a small, little-neighborhood environment." He pointed out that some of the people he went to high school with had never even set foot in Manhattan. That was not the life Hank Greenberg wanted.

3

——◆·◆·◆——

Greenberg's Time

I am alert to discrimination. I grew up during
World War II in a Jewish family. I have memories
as a child, even before the war, of being in a car
with my parents and passing a place in Pennsylvania,
a resort with a sign out in front that read: "No dogs
or Jews allowed." Signs of that kind existed in this
country during my childhood. One couldn't help
but be sensitive to discrimination living as a Jew
in America at the time of World War II.
—Supreme Court Justice Ruth Bader Ginsburg
at her Senate confirmation hearings in response
to a question from Senator Edward Kennedy
on her sensitivity to racial discrimination

A JEW rising to prominence in America could not have chosen a more difficult time in all of American history than the
1930s. Among Jews there was a growing belief that any time a

Jew was celebrated he or she was "asking for trouble." *New York Times* publisher Arthur Hays Sulzberger and Secretary of the Treasury Henry Morgenthau were among the notable Jews who opposed the 1939 Supreme Court nomination of Felix Frankfurter on the grounds that it would provoke anti-Semitism. In 1936 Supreme Court Justice Louis Brandeis, one of two Jews on the Court, along with Benjamin Cardozo, reluctantly turned down an honorary degree from Hebrew University because, he said, "We must run no risk of raising another groundless ground for anti-Semitism."

Anti-Semitism has always been present in American society. In 1654, when Peter Stuyvesant was governor of New Amsterdam, he asked his employers, the Dutch West India Company, to exclude Jews from the colonial settlement, explaining that they were "a deceitful race." However, back in Holland, the company, having a number of Jews on its board of directors, took an unfavorable view of the request. In 1780 young John Quincy Adams, while visiting Holland, observed in his diary that Jews "would steal your eyes out of your head if they possibly could." Jefferson thought that Jews lacked ethical standards—though that assessment is much more favorable than the views he expressed on black people in *Notes on the State of Virginia*.

In the early years of American history, the negative image of Jews was largely an abstraction, since there were not many in America and few Americans had ever met one. The word *Jew* was used as a pejorative term for a loathsome, dishonest person—not necessarily an actual Jew. When political enemies labeled President John Tyler a Jew, they were suggesting not that he was Jewish but that he was despicable. Even into the twentieth century in America the word *Jew* was still considered an insult, and respected Jewish public figures, including Hank Greenberg, were often referred to as Hebrews instead.

During World War I and its aftermath, anti-Semitism

flourished along with a broader xenophobia, as the brutal war was seen by many as the inevitable price of foreign involvement. While Moe Berg was studying modern languages at Princeton, the state of Nebraska passed a law making it illegal to teach foreign languages in any school in the state, public or private. Anti-immigrant and anti-immigration sentiment soared, and this went hand in hand with anti-Semitism because Jews were seen as the ultimate foreigners. An almost obsessive fear of communism after the Russian Revolution also translated into a deep distrust of Jews throughout America.

In 1921 Congress passed a law limiting immigration to 3 percent of the existing population of any group as counted in the 1910 census. In 1924 it was decided that the previous immigration law had been too liberal, and Congress lowered the quota to 2 percent and based it on the 1890 census. Two percent of the total 1890 population of fewer than half a million Jews meant that fewer than ten thousand Jewish immigrants could enter the country per year. By the end of the decade even tighter quotas were in place. Only slightly more lenient terms were allowed for German, Irish, and British immigrants, but even the German quota was not enough for the half million German Jews in desperate need in the 1930s.

In the 1920s leading universities, which had been admitting increasing numbers of Jews—motivated in some cases by a desire to improve their basketball teams—started worrying that too many were getting in. Certainly 22 percent of the Harvard student body was a far too high Jewish representation for the comfort of the president, Abbott Lawrence Lowell, who suggested cutting down the number of Jews accepted. Lowell had also written President Woodrow Wilson, urging him not to appoint Brandeis to the Supreme Court. In 1922, the year Lowell suggested cutting the Jewish quota, the New York lawyer Franklin Delano Roosevelt, a member of the Harvard Board of Overseers, expressed a similar concern and helped devise a plan to decrease the percentage of Jewish admissions to the university by about 2 points a year until Jewish attendance at Harvard was reduced to 15 percent. Yale, Princeton, the University of Pennsylvania, and Columbia also moved to reduce the number of Jews among their students.

In the 1920s and 1930s property deeds often included language restricting the owner from selling to a black or a Jew. Jewish faculty members at leading universities were a rarity, as were Jewish doctors at leading hospitals. It was extremely difficult for a Jew to get a position with the State Department, and even in New York City, where the population was one-fourth Jewish, few Jews were getting top jobs. In fact, compared with most professions at the time, baseball seemed surprisingly open to Jews.

Greenberg's rookie season, 1933, was a particularly bad year for the Jewish people. In Germany, Adolf Hitler came to power, and the Nazis' assertion that Jews were the source of Germany's economic woes resonated with many Depression-era Americans looking for a scapegoat. Some of Franklin Roosevelt's detractors referred to the New Deal as the "Jew Deal," attributing the president's economic policies to Jews close to him. Some even spread the rumor that Roosevelt himself was Jewish and had changed his name from Rosenvelt.

Once the United States went to war with Germany in 1941, expressions of support for the Nazis became an act of treason. But in the 1930s favorable attitudes toward the Nazis were not uncommon among fundamentalist Christians and other conservatives, who frequently cited Hitler's abstention from tobacco and alcohol as evidence of his upstanding character.

Some Christian leaders rallied to the support of Jews. In 1933 the minister of New York's Riverside Church, Harry Emerson Fosdick, circulated a petition signed by twelve hundred clergymen protesting the Nazis' brutal mistreatment of

Jews, calling it "a cold pogrom of inconceivable cruelty." Others spoke out as well, including John L. Lewis, leader of the Congress of Industrial Organizations (CIO), who called for a complete boycott of Germany, an idea rejected by American corporations, which were selling American industrial products to the new Germany's rebuilding effort.

While there were large anti-Nazi protests in the United States, there were also pro-Nazi demonstrations and even an active American Nazi party. Jewish shops and synagogues were being vandalized in American cities including New York and Boston. Not all support for the Nazis came from marginal figures. The nation's most popular hero, following his 1927 solo transatlantic flight, was Charles Lindbergh. The twenty-five-year-old pilot in his single-seat, single-engine, linen-covered plane had succeeded where at least six predecessors had died trying. He had conquered the Atlantic Ocean, leading the way to a new century in which flight would become commonplace, and in so doing he had generated even more excitement for the frenetically exciting 1920s. Almost everyone, including Hank Greenberg in at least one interview, named Lindbergh as the biggest star of the age. But the 1930s revealed a different side to Lindbergh. The aviator spent time in Germany studying aviation and became friendly with Hermann Göring, commander in chief of Hitler's Luftwaffe. In 1938 Göring presented Lindbergh with a German medal of honor. Lindbergh had great affection for "Nordic people," and in the late 1930s he expressed regret that Americans and their fellow Nordics, the Germans, were at odds. Once the war began Lindbergh fell out of favor. The military denied his enlistment because of his Nazi sympathies.

In signing with the Tigers because they paid well and Detroit "was a good baseball town" with a good hitters' park, Greenberg had chosen the city that Louis Brandeis, who had traveled the country in the course of his legal career, regarded as the most anti-Semitic in the United States. By 1930, when Greenberg came to town to play his first major league game, Detroit had grown from a town of 200,000 at the turn of the century to the fourth-largest city in the nation, with a population of almost a million people, of whom approximately 50,000 were Jewish.

Most of the Jewish population had settled in a thirty-block ghetto centered around Hastings Street off of East Grand Boulevard, where there were as many as twenty synagogues. But by the 1930s, in a process common to American cities, Jews had started moving out of the most densely populated urban areas, to be replaced by a fast-growing black population.

It was a bad omen for the rookie New York Jew that Jews were excluded from clubs and athletic organizations in Detroit, though this was also sometimes true in New York. Detroit was home to the two most notorious and virulent anti-Semites in America: Henry Ford and Charles Coughlin. It was not by chance that once hostilities with Germany became imminent and Lindbergh became an outcast because of his sympathies, he could still get a job with Henry Ford in Detroit. It was common knowledge that no Jewish doctor could work at the Detroit hospital run by Henry Ford. In 1919 Ford bought a small weekly newspaper, the *Dearborn Independent*, with a circulation of about 70,000. Ford sold the paper for five cents an issue with the slogan under the masthead, "Chronicler of the Neglected Truth." Much of Ford's neglected truth was anti-Semitic, often resurrecting old hate diatribes from Europe. In May 1920 the *Independent* ran an article based on *The Protocols of the Elders of Zion*, a nineteenth-century European hoax that purported to describe an international plot by Jews to take over the world. The Ford version was called "The International Jew: The World's Problem." For ninety-one editions the newspaper featured an anti-Semitic attack each week. And regular attacks continued periodically after that. Within two years the paper had increased its circulation ten times to 700,000, making it one of the most popular papers in the United States.

The *Independent*'s series was translated and circulated in continental Europe, where it accompanied the rise of Nazism. A number of biographies and articles on Ford depict the series as an important influence on Hitler's *Mein Kampf*. In any event, Hitler placed a portrait of Ford on the wall of his office, called him "my inspiration," and bestowed upon him Germany's highest honor for which non-Germans were eligible. The German Consul in Cleveland traveled to Detroit to present the award to Ford at his seventy-fifth birthday party.

Yet Ford did not appear to understand why Jews were offended. He offered a car to Rabbi Franklin and seemed perplexed when the rabbi refused to accept it. Most American Jews refused to buy Ford products, and Jewish Hollywood producers and directors avoided using Fords unless the script called for a car to break down. The Detroit historian Irwin Cohen recalled a popular joke that circulated among Jews in the 1920s. Henry Ford goes to a fortune-teller and is told that he will die on a Jewish holiday. Ford wants to know which holiday—Rosh Hashanah? Yom Kippur? Passover? Chanukah?

The fortune-teller says, "Mr. Ford, any day you die will be a Jewish holiday."

Father Charles Coughlin was a Detroit Catholic priest from a suburb that was infamous for its Ku Klux Klan connections. With a silvery radio voice he gained a following in the 1930s by denouncing the economic forces that he said were causing the Depression. His early broadcasts made thinly veiled references to Jews, but by 1935 the veil was off. In one broadcast he raged, "When we get through with the Jews in America, they'll think the treatment they received in Germany was nothing."

Coughlin grew increasingly virulent in his anti-Semitism,

and the more vicious he got, the more listeners he gained. By the late 1930s he was a national figure, railing against the Jews with an estimated twenty million to thirty million listeners tuning into his broadcasts. As the Nazis grew more brutal, he was their apologist. According to Coughlin, the Nazis were just trying to defend themselves from the Jews, who had destroyed their economy, and to stop the communists. Coughlin vaguely expressed regret for Nazi "excesses" but continued to maintain that it was really the Jews' own fault. Most important, he exhorted America not to let sympathy translate into allowing Jewish refugees into the United States. Polls at the time indicated that the public largely agreed with Coughlin that the Jews had brought about their own mistreatment. Polls also showed that more than half of Americans believed Jews to be greedy and dishonest. An overwhelming majority of Americans did not want Jewish refugees from the Nazis to be admitted into the United States.

In September 2010 the previously unknown diaries of the U.S. diplomat James McDonald came to light, revealing that he returned from a trip to Germany in 1933 and expressed deep concern to Roosevelt about the fate of Jews there. Roosevelt told McDonald that he would send Germany a warning, but he never did. In September of that year Judge Irving Lehman, brother of the New York governor, and secretary of the treasury and architect of the New Deal Henry Morgenthau Jr. met with the president and urged him to speak in defense of the Jews. Roosevelt said that it would be better to speak of a general deterioration in human rights in Germany and not specifically to mention the Jews. But he never did that, either. Nor did the president respond to the pleas of an eyewitness to Nazi brutality, Alice Hamilton, brought to him by his wife, Eleanor Roosevelt. During that entire first year of Nazi rule Rabbi Stephen Wise of the American Jewish Congress repeatedly urged the administration to speak out on behalf of German

Jews. On October 15 Wise wrote that the only response from the White House was "indifference and unconcern."

Despite the claim of anti-Semites that the Roosevelt administration was controlled by Jews, the administration was indifferent to the pleas of American Jews and their organizations to rescue their European counterparts. Some historians have speculated that the policy was designed to disprove the anti-Semites' claim. It was clear to Roosevelt that if he was to rally Americans to go to war with Germany, saving the Jews would not be a popular cause. Father Coughlin, who opposed the war, asked, "Must the entire world go to war for 600,000 Jews in Germany?" And so the Nazis, who were watching for a world outcry, had no real pressure from England, France, or the United States to change their policies toward Jews. Few besides Jews and leftists actively opposed the Nazis from the start. Many, including Winston Churchill, praised the fascist movement for its strength in standing up to communism. Churchill was impressed by Hitler at their 1935 meeting, which he described in his 1937 book *Great Contemporaries*, calling Hitler "a highly competent, cool, well-informed functionary with an agreeable manner [and] a disarming smile," and predicted that in time Hitler would become "a gentler figure." Perhaps former British Prime Minister David Lloyd George spoke with more candor in 1933 when Hitler came to power. Lloyd George cautioned against overthrowing the new German dictator, saying that a deposed Führer would be replaced by "extreme Communism. Surely that cannot be our objective."

In September 1921 Ford's *Dearborn Independent* ran an article complaining about the excessive number of Jews in sports with the front-page headline "The Peril of Baseball—'Too Much Jew.'" Ford claimed that though Jews had a small presence in baseball and there were no Jews on the Tigers at the time, all the problems of baseball could be summed up in those last three words "Too much Jew." Oddly, the article itself began by undercutting that premise with a contradictory stereotype:

> To begin with, Jews are not sportsmen. This is not set down in complaint against them, but merely as analysis. It may be a defect in their character, or it may not; it is nevertheless a fact which discriminating Jews unhesitatingly acknowledge. Whether this is due to their physical lethargy, their dislike of unnecessary physical action, or their serious cast of mind, others may decide.
>
> The Jew is not naturally an out-of-door sportsman.

But if the anti-Semites had trouble getting their story straight, fifty thousand Detroit Jews, not all of them baseball fans, rejoiced when a six-foot-four-inch slugger named Greenberg started smacking balls out of Navin Field.

4

Becoming Hank

> Our accents disappeared. Our strides became quick
> and confident. My left-handedness, regarded by my
> parents as a devil's curse, turned to my advantage
> in the pitcher's box. I threw a submarine ball,
> my knuckles grazing the dirt as I released it.
> "Get those knuckles dirty, Jackie!"
> my infielders would shout—
> Jackie, not Yakov.
> —Eric Rolfe Greenberg, *The Celebrant*

At the time Hank Greenberg received his first paycheck of $6,000 as a major league baseball player, the average annual income in the United States was $1,970, and the average cost of a new car was $640. Greenberg, always serious about the management of his money, invested it in tobacco stock. If he had sold the next day, he would have made an $800 profit. But this was September 1929, and with the market climbing to unprecedented heights, it seemed prudent to hold onto his stock. A month later the biggest crash in the history of the market obliterated Greenberg's investment, along with those of millions of others. That crash defined the most important decade of Greenberg's major league career, but for him the loss of his money was dwarfed by the thrilling fact that he was going off to play professional baseball.

The train ride to the Tigers' spring training camp in Tampa, Florida, early in 1930, was the longest trip Greenberg had ever taken, his first journey away from the Northeast. When he got there, at the age of nineteen and fresh out of the Bronx, he was put up in the luxurious Tampa Bay Hotel, a kid in the company of mature men he had learned about in the papers, stars like second baseman Charlie Gehringer, outfielder Harry Rice, and pitcher Waite Hoyt. The pros barely spoke to the rookie. It has always been that way in baseball. New recruits are brought up to replace veterans, and no one wants to see the towering nineteen-year-old who is being groomed for his job.

"They were all grown men, well-groomed and well-dressed," he noted many years later. Their dress made a lasting impression, and expensive and elegant clothing was to become a Greenberg trademark. Teammates commented on the $35 Sulka ties he wore at the height of the Depression, when Sulka was known as the haberdasher of the wealthy—including, ironically, Henry Ford.

The hotel was in the grand Moorish style with domes and arches, the kind of romantic Mediterranean architecture for which Florida resorts became famous in the twenties. According to Greenberg, the wealthy clientele was very surprised to find baseball players in its midst. First-class accommodations for baseball players were unusual in 1929, when ballplayers, by today's standards, were neither highly paid nor pampered.

Greenberg reported to spring training as Henry Greenberg. He did not want to play professional baseball as Hymie, a name he never used again. Once he became a pro ballplayer even his family started calling him Henry or Hank. He had already used the name Henry on his application to the 92nd Street Y, a context where Hymie would have been easily accepted. It seems probable that the new name, like the better clothes, was an attempt to become more worldly rather than to cover up his Jewishness. Greenberg never tried to conceal his ethnic identity. Even when he decided to take a middle name because he thought that would make him seem more urbane, he chose that of his brother, Benjamin, a Jewish name.

Hank probably knew that he would face some anti-Semitism playing baseball away from New York. Other Jewish athletes had already experienced it. The star Jewish basketball players of the 1920s sometimes found makeshift coffins or nooses on display, or graffiti reading "Kill the Christ killer." They heard shouted epithets and dodged thrown objects. Life was no easier on the baseball diamond. In the 1920s, when Andy Cohen was playing in the minor leagues, a heckler kept shouting "Christ killer" at him. Finally Cohen approached the grandstand, bat in hand, and shouted to his tormentor, "Come down here and I'll kill you too."

Nor did Jewish players have a monopoly on abuse. Italians, Poles—almost any player perceived to have an ethnic background was apt to be harassed. *Life* magazine praised Joe DiMaggio because he "never reeked of garlic." But the harassment of Jews was especially vitriolic. Some verses of "Cohen at the Bat," the popular rhyme that greeted Andy Cohen wherever he played, had distinctly anti-Semitic overtones:

> And from the stands and bleachers
> The cry of "oye, oye," rose,
> And up came Andy Cohen half a
> Foot behind his nose.

Hank had faced anti-Semitism before. He had seen it as a small child in lower Manhattan and then later at James Monroe High School, which was in a different part of the Bronx from Crotona Park. Of course, being one of the biggest, strongest kids around had an impact on how he dealt with it. Al Kirchenstein, six years younger than Hank, had an older brother Sidney who attended James Monroe with the future baseball star. Kirchenstein said that although he never met Greenberg, he remembered hearing about him from Sidney. "I just remember that they were two tough kids. Whenever anybody made anti-Semitic remarks they made them stop. [The hecklers] were afraid of them. . . . They made sure those kids never said that again." Throughout his life, *tough* was a word frequently used by Hank's friends to describe him. Whether such incidents ever happened in high school or not, this was the reputation Greenberg left behind in the Bronx. It is better documented that more than once as a major league player, Greenberg took a similar stand. He was a large, tough kid without any real strategy for facing anti-Semitism other than standing down anyone who insulted him or his people.

After an unremarkable spring training, Greenberg was sent to a Class A team—roughly the middle level of the minor leagues—in Hartford, Connecticut. He was still inexperienced, his footwork at first base was clumsy, he missed fly balls, and even his batting was unspectacular. To his disappointment, after only seventeen games in Hartford, he was sent down to a Class C team in Raleigh, North Carolina. He had never experienced such a sports failure. A great competitor, he always improved after a setback. He committed himself to turning things around. It meant still more and more hours of practice, but the result was that in Raleigh he first distinguished himself as a hitter in professional baseball.

The only Jew on the team, not to mention one of the few

players from an urban background, Hank began to realize how far he was from the Jewish world he had grown up in. In his autobiography he later said of his experience in North Carolina, "I encountered some hostility, but I'd say much more curiosity than hostility." One teammate stared at him because he had never seen a Jew before, and after a good, hard look was surprised to discover that a Jew didn't appear to be any different from other people. Hank's roommate from Atlanta seemed genuinely surprised that he didn't have horns.

It was also in Raleigh that Hank first began to see that if he succeeded as a baseball player, his success would hold special significance in Jewish communities. One local Jew fixed Greenberg up with his daughter. This was the first date nineteen-year-old Hank had ever been on. The evening, though uneventful, introduced him to the two new roles baseball would lead him into—Jewish icon and heartthrob. He had not anticipated either one. Though he grew into a strikingly handsome man, he had spent his high school years too large and awkward to have much success with girls. Later, when he was a star, the shy, awkward boy could at times still be seen underneath the handsome, well-dressed celebrity.

Greenberg did so well for the team that when Raleigh's season ended, the Tigers brought him up to Detroit for the final three weeks of the major league season. He arrived in his spanking new Model A Ford that he had bought in Raleigh for $375, and was devoted to keeping cleaned and waxed. That he could buy a Ford in 1930 at the height of the controversy over Henry Ford's anti-Semitism shows how removed from the Jewish world and Jewish issues he was.

It had been another lackluster season for the Tigers, who were ending it in fifth place out of eight teams in the league and had nothing to lose. Tiger scout Jean Dubuc proposed that they give Greenberg a taste of the majors. But it wasn't easy for the young upstart. His locker was next to that of Waite Hoyt, a fellow New Yorker who had been a top pitcher for the Yankees in the golden age of Babe Ruth. Greenberg reported in his autobiography that in three weeks of dressing and undressing side by side, Hoyt never said a single word to him. Nor did most of the other men. Remembering his discomfort at this silent treatment, when Greenberg became a star, he broke with tradition and went to great lengths to welcome and encourage rookies.

When Hank Greenberg finally got his first major league at-bat, he was terrified. He was sent in as a pinch hitter in a hopeless losing game against the Yankees. The pitcher was Red Ruffing, the future Hall of Fame strikeout pitcher. "I was scared to death," he recalled in his autobiography. "I knelt in the on-deck circle and looked out at Yankees like Babe Ruth and Lou Gehrig and Ben Chapman and Bill Dickey and Lyn Lary and said to myself, 'What am I doing here?'"

He could never remember what kind of pitch he swung at, but said, "I was as good as out before I ever reached the plate." In fact, he hit a modest pop-up which was effortlessly caught by third baseman Tony Lazzeri. And that was it. Hank Greenberg's first major league at-bat was over.

Many great players start their careers with easy outs, and Greenberg resolved that he would do better next time. But the season was winding down and there was no next time, not in 1930. Manager Bucky Harris simply wasn't playing him, and the nineteen-year-old Greenberg was growing increasingly frustrated. Still youthful himself, Harris was already a baseball legend. In 1924, when he was only twenty-seven and the youngest manager in the major leagues, he took the chronically last-place Washington Senators to the World Series against the New York Giants. As both a player and manager he was pivotal in leading Washington to its only championship. He was a consistent hitter and a good fielder, but he earned a reputation as an exceptionally savvy manager, making sudden and unpredictable shifts that proved brilliant. During the 1924 World Series he mystified fans and management when he started his fourth-best pitcher, right-hander Curly Ogden, in the decisive game 7 of the series. But by starting an unimpressive right-hander he guaranteed that the Giants would play left-handed-hitting Bill Terry, who was hitting over .400 in the series. Terry was a future Hall of Famer remembered along with Greenberg and Gehrig as one of the great first basemen. But at the time the rookie was not hitting left-handed pitchers. After Ogden had faced only two batters, striking out the first and walking the second, Harris took him out of the game and put in George Mogridge, a lefty. This neutralized Terry and eventually forced John McGraw to take him out of the Giants' lineup. Not only did the Senators win the series but young Bucky Harris had out-managed the great McGraw. It was risky after that to second-guess Harris. Traded to the Tigers after the 1928 season, Harris, though only thirty-one, stopped playing to devote himself entirely to managing.

Finally, in the eighth inning of the final game of the season, Harris called Greenberg to first base. But Greenberg refused to play. He stormed off the field, got dressed, slid into his shiny Ford, and headed for New York. No one cared. The club never even commented on it. Greenberg was not important.

For a man who almost always behaved well, this was a surprising beginning. But Greenberg never had misgivings about leaving the field during the game, an act completely contrary to the unspoken professional code of baseball. Even at the end of his life, when describing this incident he defiantly stated, "That's how I felt and that's what I did. And I never had any regrets." To Greenberg, being brought up to the majors just to sit on the bench was a bully's tease, an unwarranted abuse, and he always believed that he should not tolerate abuse. In time he would learn to moderate his temper, but the defiant streak always remained just under the surface.

Back in the Bronx, Hank did not seem troubled by the incident. He was now the neighborhood's "major leaguer." One at-bat in one game qualified him, and, in fact, there are numerous major leaguers in the record book whose career was no longer than a single at-bat.

His parents, as they would say, *kvelled;* they were proud of their boy, the neighborhood hero. But Greenberg was still yearning for more than just being the hero of his neighborhood. In *At Home in America,* Deborah Dash Moore wrote about second-generation New York Jews who, no longer linked by the immigrant experience like the previous generation, worked in "Jewish industries" that reinforced their Jewish identity. Working in these industries was not a choice they made to preserve their Jewishness. In an age of anti-Semitism and economic crisis, these were simply the jobs that were available to Jews. "Jews were linked by concentration in such industries as the garment trades," Moore writes. This was true of Hank's older brother Ben, his sister Lillian, and later on, after a brief fling with minor league baseball, his younger brother Joe. But that was not to be Hank Greenberg's world. He wanted something larger.

Hank Greenberg, the major league baseball player, still lived in the Bronx, but he wasn't limited by it. He kept his Ford polished and regularly drove into Manhattan at a time when such a trip was unusual in his neighborhood. He dressed in expensive suits and dined in Midtown restaurants, and went to the theater and to movies in Times Square. He also went into Manhattan to play handball indoors at the 92nd Street Y, to keep in shape after the weather became cold. One day, after running a traffic light, he was stopped by a burly Irish policeman who asked his profession and then laughed at the seemingly preposterous idea that a kid named Greenberg could be a professional baseball player. But Hank felt that he was at last on his way. "I felt I was becoming a man of the world," he said in his autobiography.

Greenberg understood that money made this new man possible. He was an unusually tough and skilled negotiator for a ballplayer. Once he was an established star, his negotiations were based on consistent hitting that had helped turn the Tigers from a losing team into a perennial contender. But barely out of his teens, with a pop-up in his sole big league at-bat, he had little leverage. He was just a minor leaguer with a good rookie year in Class C ball. Yet he still bargained hard, getting under Tiger owner Frank Navin's skin in the process. Greenberg first irritated Navin by denouncing Bucky Harris for not playing him after his promotion. Navin retorted that the rookie had been given an opportunity to experience the major league atmosphere; the team had been under no obligation to let him play. "It seems to me," Navin wrote to young Green-berg, "it comes with rather poor grace from a boy who has just made good in Class C to criticize a manager of Harris' well-known ability." Navin told the rookie that he could either ac-cept the offer or leave.

The twenty-year-old Greenberg's bluff had been called: he packed up his Ford and drove for five days to report to Beau-mont, Texas. Beaumont was a Class A team, two steps up from Raleigh but still three steps down from the majors. It was in the Texas League, a hard-playing league that had produced many major leaguers, including Dizzy and Paul Dean and Andy Cohen. But Greenberg did not last long in Beaumont. The team had a more skilled and experienced first baseman on the roster, so Greenberg was sent to play for the Class B Evansville Hubs in Indiana. Evansville was not even a dominant team in the Three-I—Illinois, Indiana, Iowa—League. Greenberg was once again disappointed and probably worried about his future. Most baseball careers die in the minor leagues, and if he did not do well in Evansville, he could be back in the Bronx with one pop-up in Detroit as the high point of a brief career. But once again he dealt with his disappointment and worry by not only practicing his hitting but obsessively working on his fielding, too. Though he made errors and never did become a great fielder, he became a competent professional first baseman. In Evansville he hit 15 home runs and batted .318. The Tiger organization was beginning to see the ballplayer he could become.

Greenberg recalled this as a happy period in his life. He enjoyed the five-hour bus rides with the team to away games, singing songs like "The Sidewalks of New York" and on the way home drinking bootlegged beer in defiance of Prohibition. He was so fond of the Tonnemacher family, in whose boarding house he lived, that when he went to the majors, he made a point of getting them tickets when Detroit was playing in Chicago or St. Louis.

But a pattern emerged and followed him from Evansville back to Texas and into Detroit. As a player and later a general manager, he spent the better part of twenty years on the receiving end of anti-Semitic abuse in ballparks. They called him kike, sheenie, a pants presser, Christ killer; they shouted about Moses and pork chops, trying to get a rise out of him with the vicious and the ridiculous. "Every ballpark I went to there'd be somebody in the stands who spent the whole afternoon just calling me, you know, names," Greenberg told the American Jewish Committee in a lengthy 1980 interview that was part of the organization's oral Jewish history project. He understood it for what it was, baiting. "To them it's a game," Greenberg said. "It's like certain people who go to the zoo to put a stick into the animals' cages to see how they can agitate them, and to some people, that's their pleasure in going to a ballpark."

This hazing came not only from fans but from players on the opposing team as well. Greenberg said, "If you're having a good day, you don't give a damn. But if you're having a bad day, why, pretty soon it gets you hot under the collar."

And on the wrong day, this powerful young man found it hard to resist a physical response. Or sometimes even on a "good day," as he described the time in 1931 when Evansville was playing in Decatur, Illinois. The third baseman had poked at him all afternoon with one epithet after another. Then the fans joined in, and every provocation from the third baseman stirred up the fans a little more. Finally, Greenberg let loose with a long round punch at the third baseman. The crowd was infuriated that he had attacked the anti-Semite, and the police were called to get the large Jew off the field. The next day's edition of the local paper, which Greenberg kept for years, ran the headline, "FANS CHARGE FIGHTING BALL PLAYER." After a number of these incidents it became clear to Greenberg that such public displays of anger only provoked anti-Semites and gained him neither respect nor peace.

The following year Greenberg was called back to Beaumont. The team had been disappointed in its first baseman, had struggled through a losing season, and needed new blood. The fields were broiling hot by day, the rippling heat making the batted and thrown ball hard to read. Night games buzzed with Texas-size mosquitoes. But there was a big league feel to the Texas League, to the quality of play, especially the pitching, even to the travel—by train rather than bus. Some of the trains may have been meant for livestock, with a few passenger cars added for the team, but it was still the first time Greenberg had ever played for a team that traveled by train, which was how the big leaguers did it.

Despite the continued taunts, Greenberg was voted the Most Valuable Player in the Texas League for the 1932 season. Having hit 39 home runs and driven in 131 runs, he was one of several players from the Beaumont team who were asked to report to spring training with the Tigers the next season. But spring training was another tryout, and it did not go well for

Greenberg. Bucky Harris was still managing, and he had signed a first baseman, Harry Davis, for a great deal of money. Davis, from Louisiana and popularly known as "Stinky," was the reverse of Greenberg, a great fielder with no power at bat. Harris sent Greenberg to third base, which he did not know how to play, and his awkwardness stood out. He threw too hard. He didn't know when to cover the base. The press used adjectives such as "large" and "sweaty" to describe him.

But the Tigers were building a hard-hitting team, and they recognized the potential of Greenberg's swing. So in the spring of 1933, Hank Greenberg's major league career began in earnest. By baseball standards, three years in the minors is a meteoric rise, but for Hank, it seemed as if it had been a long road.

When the team went north to start the season, the smooth-fielding Davis was on first and Greenberg sat on the bench. To keep in shape, he played in pickup games at Belle Isle Park, on an island in the Detroit River. He always found a way to work on his game and stay in shape. It was exciting to be in the majors at last, but he remembered his past experience with the frustratingly inscrutable Harris and wondered how much he would get to play.

Two weeks into the season Harris put him into a game against St. Louis. It was his chance to show Harris and the organization how he could hit. But he couldn't hit left-handed Lloyd Brown that day in three at-bats against him, and he went back to the bench. But a week later, when he was put in against Brown again, he got a hit, and the Tigers began to use him more, especially against left-handed pitchers. On May 6, against the Washington Senators, he batted against Earl Whitehill, one of the most intimidating pitchers in the game. A former Tiger, Whitehill won 218 games in a long career—and hit 101 batters with pitches. Greenberg hit his first home run against him. He had broken through.

Twenty days later, Greenberg got his second home run,

against another accomplished left-handed pitcher, Rube Walberg of the Philadelphia Athletics. Soon home runs started to become a habit, especially against lefty pitchers. Conventional baseball wisdom holds that it is easier for a right-handed batter to hit a left-handed pitcher because the pitch comes from the opposite side of the plate from where the batter swings, and he is therefore in position to follow the ball without moving his head. But because lefties are less common than righties, batters get less experience against them, so being able to hit left-handers well is a valuable asset.

Greenberg relentlessly practiced hitting, both as a muscle-building exercise and as a way of working on his timing. That first full season, 1933, he hit 12 home runs, which was a respectable, even promising, total. But more important, his batting average was .301, just above the accepted threshold for hitting prowess. He had had a good rookie season, securing his place on the Tigers. Stinky Davis would be back in the minor leagues in 1934, while Hank Greenberg played every game but that famous one on Yom Kippur. Instead of a hotel where he had to hang his clothes on the shower rod, as in the minor leagues, he found himself in the Detroit Leland, where they had not only closets but a restaurant with a full orchestra. He loved being a baseball player and being a part of the team. A young man out of New York, he was fascinated by many of the other players, country boys whose "whole life experience was with animals and they knew how animals lived—how they copulated, what they ate, how they behaved," he said in his autobiography. "They saw the whole pattern of life in terms of animals and crops and soil." Midwest baseball was a great adventure for a rookie from the Bronx.

Jews were not new to sports in Detroit when Greenberg arrived. In 1932, a year before Greenberg became a full-time Tiger, the University of Michigan's star quarterback, Harry

Newman, was a Detroit Jew, and Izzy Goldstein, three years older than Greenberg and raised only about two blocks away in the Bronx, was pitching for the Tigers.

Nor were the Tigers the only major league team at the time with Jewish players. Moe Berg was still catching for the Senators. Outfielder Morris Arnovich started with the Phillies two years after Greenberg became the Tigers' full-time first baseman. From a rabbinical family, Arnovich continued to keep a kosher diet throughout his major league career and after. Catcher Harry Danning, who came up with the Giants in 1933, batted .300 as a full-time player three consecutive seasons starting in 1938. In 1934 the Florida hotel where the Giants stayed during spring training refused to give rooms to Danning and Phil Weintraub, a first baseman and outfielder, and another solid hitter. Led by first baseman Bill Terry, the entire team threatened to leave, forcing the hotel to reverse its policy.

Numerous Jews were playing baseball during Greenberg's era, as the public realized in 1938 when the Phillies had a doubleheader scheduled in Boston on Rosh Hashanah. After the famous Greenberg Yom Kippur incident of 1934, the press was poised to report on whether the Phillies' three Jewish players would play when the holiday conflicted with a game. For Arnovich there was no agonizing, because, unlike Greenberg, he was genuinely religious. Weintraub decided that he would not play either. How could you, after Greenberg's gesture, if you wanted to keep your Jewish fans? But Eddie Feinberg, just shy of his twenty-first birthday, recently called up from the minors, and eager to build his career, decided to play. For the rest of his life, he said that he regretted that decision, a regret which may have been influenced by the fact that in those two games, in eight at-bats, he did not get a single hit.

An older Greenberg, reflecting on his career, told the American Jewish Committee, "I think when I broke into the major leagues I was the only Jewish player in baseball." Of course, he knew the other Jewish players, especially the ones he played against in the American League. There was later even another Jew with him on the Tigers, Harry Eisenstat, who made an impression on Greenberg on the final day of the season in 1938 by outpitching Cleveland's Bob Feller, whom Greenberg, among many others, regarded as the toughest pitcher in baseball.

Yet when Hank Greenberg looked back on those years, he remembered being alone. Not given to hyperbole and never boastful, Greenberg must have genuinely felt isolated. And in some ways, he might as well have been the only Jew in the majors because he was the one the spotlight never left.

From 1871 to the beginning of the twenty-first century, there were roughly 140 Jewish major league players, representing less than 1 percent of the total 16,700 players—even though Jews averaged about 3 percent of the American population over those years. When the size of the Jewish population is taken into account, a greater percentage played baseball in the nineteenth century, when fewer than 100,000 Jews lived in the United States, than in the first half of the twentieth century, when the Jewish population was well over two million. But a smaller percentage of the Jews of Greenberg's generation were fully assimilated than was true of the Jewish population— or the Jewish baseball population—of the nineteenth century.

Although Greenberg saw himself as an assimilated Jew, a baseball player who happened to be Jewish, the public did not see him that way; from the outside, Jews were Jews, assimilated or not, and they were seen as a people apart. But Greenberg was certainly not the stereotypical Jewish baseball player. He was not in the mold of Moe Berg, for instance, the "good field, no hit" journeyman who spent much of his spare time studying.

Hank Greenberg had a lot of hit—that was the striking thing about his game. Robert Steinberg, a Detroit Jew born in 1931, whose uncle was a close friend of Greenberg's, still has the signed ball Hank gave him when he was seven years old.

Asked why Greenberg was so revered by American Jews when there were numerous other Jewish players, Steinberg went through the usual litany—Hank was part of the community, he respected the Jewish holidays—and then he paused. "And he hit a hell of a lot of home runs."

Hitting home runs is the single most popular act in the game of baseball. This fact, which has always been true, was reaffirmed in a 2009 ESPN/Seton Hall poll in which 30 percent of respondents who identified themselves as sports fans said that home runs were their favorite events in baseball. Baseball aficionados talk about a duel between two great pitchers who send the game scoreless into extra innings, or the great over-the-shoulder outfield catch that saves the game, about the unassisted double play, the steal of home. Baseball is a subtle game with innumerable shifts and strategies. But when a player steps up to the plate, swings the bat, and sends the ball over the outfield wall, the prospects for both teams have been significantly altered by a simple clear act that everyone understands.

Hank Greenberg himself thought too much was made of home runs. As he frequently complained to the press, "Everybody remembers me for hitting 58 home runs. Nobody remembers me for having hit 183 runs batted in." He insisted that driving in runs was more important than hitting home runs. Probably most managers would agree, but not the owners. Home runs are the better box-office draw.

In 1873 Lipman Pike led his league in home runs by hitting 4. Until 1919 baseball produced few home runs, and the game was characterized by fast, artful base running, daringly stolen bases, ingeniously placed soft hits that got the batter to first base, and hit-and-run strategies intended to move runners one base closer to home. This was the "dead ball era," and the ball that was used did, in fact, lack life. But the style of play was a function less of the equipment and more of the prevailing strategy of the game. The 1906 Chicago White Sox, known as "The Hitless Wonders," won the World Series from the Cubs in six games despite having the lowest team batting average in the American League. In 1908 the White Sox were still a close contender for the American League pennant even though the entire team hit only 3 home runs for the season. Detroit's Sam Crawford hit 7 home runs that season—and led the American League. The year before, Harry Davis of the Philadelphia Athletics, no relation to the Harry "Stinky" Davis whom Greenberg later replaced, won his fourth consecutive AL home run title by slugging 8.

Then Babe Ruth appeared. In 1919, while still pitching part-time, he hit 29 home runs, the most ever hit by a player in a season to date, besting Ned Williamson's 1884 season record of 27. Home runs in a season instantly became the most celebrated record in a game of records. Ruth's home runs not only changed the financial standing of the struggling New York Yankees but, in so doing, changed the game of baseball. In an age when baseball earned most of its income from ticket sales at the ballpark, people packed in to see the Yankees because they wanted to see Babe Ruth hit one out of the park. The dead ball era was over. Every club wanted big hitters—the kind of hitters who when they step up to the plate cause the crowd to anticipate that the whole game might now change—as sports announcers like to say—"with one swing of the bat."

Hank Greenberg's career started as Ruth's was winding down and everyone was looking for "the next Babe Ruth." Although Ruth did a lot of things well, "the next Babe Ruth" meant the next great home run producer. It seemed every time a player hit a few home runs in rapid succession it was suggested that he might be the next Babe Ruth. But few players hit home runs with enough regularity to be seriously considered for the title; one who did was Hank Greenberg. Fans and sportswriters eagerly watched his every swing.

Ironically, Greenberg, who admired the strategies of the dead ball era, would not have done well in those days because he was not a good enough base runner. But his home runs were the kind everyone wants to see. First there is that deep, ripe-melon thwack. You can usually tell a good home run with your eyes shut, just by the sound of the ball on the bat. Greenberg's home runs were not line drives that miraculously cleared the back wall. When he made contact, the ball looked like it had been launched, soaring into space in a huge arc as though de-scribing the curvature of the earth.

Some of the other Jewish players were also good hitters, but they were not home run hitters like Greenberg; none was a contender for the title "the next Babe Ruth." Ruth was the biggest sports hero in the history of American sports. Wouldn't it be something if the next one were Jewish? What would the followers of Father Coughlin think of that? Wouldn't it change the whole standing of Jews in America? And wouldn't it also change the attitudes of our fathers, the immigrants who looked down on sports? That shift in thinking had already started hap-pening after Greenberg chose not to play on Yom Kippur. Roger Angell, in his 1972 book *Five Seasons*, quoted a Detroit Jew on Greenberg's hitting: "[He] made baseball acceptable to our parents, so for once they didn't mind if we took a little time off from the big process of getting into college."

When Greenberg's very Jewish face appeared on a Wheaties box, "the breakfast of champions," it seemed to Amer-ican Jews that a barrier had been lifted. Morrie Arnovich had those same *hamisch* good looks. But at five foot ten, he was called "little Moe." Greenberg was big—almost of biblical propor-tions, a Samson-like figure, or at least a ba'al guf, who arrived to defend the Jewish people at their moment of persecution. When nonagenarian Jews are asked today why Greenberg was so im-portant, the answer inevitably comes back—because there was Coughlin, because there was Ford, because there was Hitler.

For five decades Jews had made steady progress in America, but now Jewish philanthropic organizations that had grown to impressive wealth and power in the 1920s had been bankrupted by the Depression, immigrant families that had risen up from poverty were sinking back into it, and the disease of anti-Semitism that they had fled in Europe was spreading in America. In fact, the entire American dream was being called into question. Some Zionists were writing off the experiment of American democracy as a home for Jews as a failure; Jews, they said, should pack up again and move to Palestine. As Beth Wenger wrote in *New York Jews and the Great Depression*, "The mood among American Jews in the 1930s was characterized more by fear than by hope." This atmosphere surely explains why the appearance of Hank Greenberg's Jewish face on the "breakfast of champions" box meant so much.

There was an ongoing debate among Jews in the 1930s. While some Jews took great pride in the success of their own, many believed that Jews who became celebrities should conceal their Jewishness rather than stir up anti-Semitism. Many baseball players felt this way, but it was an even more strongly held belief in Hollywood, where there was an abundance of prominent Jews among producers, directors, and actors. Wouldn't it be better if Julius Garfinkle became John Garfield? And what kind of name was Emmanuel Goldenberg for a movie star? Better to call him Edward G. Robinson. Once Meshilem Meier Weisenfreund, the Yiddish theater actor, went to Hollywood, it was considered more prudent to change his name to Paul Muni, while Marion Levy became Paulette Goddard. Maybe she was French.

There were inherent contradictions: Jews and their culture were here, but they weren't here. This paradox was illustrated by the Andrews Sisters, a solidly Midwestern singing group who became famous in 1937 singing a song from Yiddish theater by Shalom Secunda with words by Jacob Jacobs, "Bei Mir

Bistu Shein": to me you are beautiful. They sang it in English, the translation provided by Sammy Cahn, who still had a Jewish name. Only the title line in regular refrains was sung in the original Yiddish, with such strong American accents that few realized it was Yiddish. Most Americans thought they were saying something like "My dear Mister Shane" or "Buy me a beer, Mister Shane." The title was presented not with Yiddish spelling but in German, "Bei Mir Bist Du Schön"; the German title helped make it popular with the Nazis, who stopped listening when they realized what it really was. It is highly doubtful whether the song would have sold a million records and made the Andrews Sisters the first female vocal group to win a gold record if those million Americans had known it was Yiddish. Having the song sung by such a conspicuously non-Jewish group—Laverne, Maxene, and Patty, Greek/Scandinavians from Minnesota—was part of the winning formula. Secunda and Jacobs had sold the song for $30, expecting it to be popular only with a handful of Jews.

Jews not only wanted to escape prejudice and be successful, they wanted other Jews to do the same. But they disagreed on how to accomplish that. Some would have been happy if their major league home run hero had changed his named to Henry Green and never said a word about Yom Kippur or anything else to do with Judaism. Numerous Jewish players were doing just that. But others argued that there had to be some Jewish heroes who everyone knew were Jewish, or young people would not want to be Jewish anymore. To them, Hammerin' Hank Greenberg, the Jewish home run hitter, was that hero.

David and Sarah Greenberg had become the celebrities of Crotona Park East, and they seemed to love their role as the parents of the Jewish star. Fans who knocked on their door would be invited in to talk, even introduced to their son if he was home. One young woman was ushered into the kitchen, and there he was—eating Wheaties. When the press interviewed the family, David typically emphasized their Orthodox household. Not only did he tell the press that he did not want his son to play on Yom Kippur in 1934, he reiterated it for Yom Kippur the following year, which coincided with game six of the 1935 World Series. Hank's mother, Sarah, was more resigned. She told the press, "I don't want him to play but he will anyway."

In fact, Hank desperately wanted to play. The Cubs had beaten the Tigers 3–0 in game one of the Series, and Hank was determined not to miss game six, in part, no doubt, because the Cubs had shouted so many anti-Semitic slurs at him from the bench in game one that the umpire, George Moriarty, ordered them to stop. They refused and an argument ensued. Commissioner Landis fined both the Cubs players and Moriarty.

In game two Detroit had come back to win 8–3, in part thanks to Greenberg's two-run homer. Playing hard, Greenberg tried to score from first base in the seventh inning. He slid head first into home plate, always a dangerous move, and slammed into Gabby Hartnett, the Cubs' catcher, snapping his left wrist. He was in intense pain, and while his parents and the press debated whether he would play on Yom Kippur, Hank was soaking his wrist alternately in very hot water and ice, hoping the swelling would go down enough for the next day's game. It cannot be known what would have happened to the myth of Hank Greenberg if the soaking had worked. But, as he found out later, his wrist was broken. He was unable to play, and this made it possible for the legend of the religious Greenberg to flourish, even though it was known that he had wanted to play. Dan Daniel of the *New York World-Telegram* wrote, "[Yesterday] was Yom Kippur, the holiest day of the year for Jews. Hank Greenberg, an Orthodox and devout believer, was eager to play, but his left wrist was so swollen he could not grip a bat." And forever after many Jews said, "Hank never played on Yom Kippur." Detroit went on to win the Series, taking three of the next four games without their slugging first baseman.

David and Sarah would go to ballgames to watch their son play, rooting for the Tigers in Detroit and other cities. They had done that even when he was in the minor leagues, spending a week in whatever small town he was playing in. Once in the majors, Greenberg was a little dismayed when he would find his father outside the ballpark signing his name in Yiddish on baseballs for perplexed kids.

The Jews in Detroit had embraced Hank as soon as he got to the majors, but the relationship was cemented in 1934 with the Yom Kippur incident. He gave talks at the synagogues and went for dinner to various homes, where neighborhood children would drop by with balls to sign. Once he heard of a boy with a broken leg who was heartbroken because he could not come over to see his hero. Greenberg went out and bought a baseball, signed it, and took it to the boy—still a much-repeated legend in the Detroit Jewish community.

But Greenberg was never comfortable with the kind of adulation he received from the Jewish community. That was why he refused the dinner in his honor after Yom Kippur in 1934. He actually came to resent the neediness of his Jewish fans, and it took him many years to understand it. He had signed on to be a baseball player, not a Jewish symbol. While he was sensitive to his responsibility to his people, the grandness of that role conflicted with his natural humility. In his autobiography he wrote, "I've never wanted to be pushed around and that was the tendency of the Jewish baseball fans in those days. Nobody was rushing to give other rookies a dinner because of their religion. I just felt funny about it and I always have. I've tried to live within the proper boundaries of my religion and have never done anything to bring discredit on Jews."

When Hank Greenberg was playing, the seats behind first base in Navin Field became a Jewish neighborhood, because that was where the fans would get the best possible view of their star. Harriet Coleman, who had a teenage crush on Greenberg, described getting a seat behind first base "where I could see him clearly and watch his every move. I knew his car. I would wait for him in the parking lot after the game." When she was thirteen, she proposed marriage. Greenberg, who tried to answer all his fan mail, wrote back that he wasn't ready—a joke, but it was probably true. In those years ballplayers did not have much of a home life, and most did not get married until after their playing careers ended. Years later, when Coleman met Greenberg at a Detroit synagogue where he was addressing a youth group, she proposed again. This time, Greenberg smiled and said, "I accept." Though he was clearly joking, Coleman still referred to it in a 2007 interview as the big event of her life. "He was such a hunk!" she said. Mary Frances Veeck, wife of his later close friend and partner Bill Veeck, said, "Hank Greenberg had the most fabulous brown eyes—eyes that you could drown in."

In Detroit, he became close to Harold and Sidney Allen, twin brothers who manufactured automobile interiors. The business world always interested Greenberg, and, unlike most people in the 1930s, he had more and more money to invest. After hitting 58 home runs in 1938, he negotiated a salary of $40,000 a year, making him not only the highest-paid player in baseball but the second highest in baseball history after Babe Ruth.

The Allen brothers would take him to the Franklin Hills Country Club, a Jewish club where he met other prominent Detroit Jews. He also became friendly with his doctor, Willard Mayer. Mayer's son Martin remembered Hank not only for his extraordinarily large hands but as a man who was under a great deal of pressure. Mayer said, "Greenberg was a very nervous, high-strung individual. My father called him 'intense.' During the World Series he couldn't sleep. He would go out to the Allen brothers' farm. Father would prescribe mild Seconal and he would go out there to try to get some sleep." This account shows how seriously Hank Greenberg took his baseball and how much pressure was on him as the Jewish star, because in other periods of his life descriptions like "happy" and "fun-loving" were more common than "intense."

The pressure he was under was not only about living up to his fans' adulation and his own expectations. Just as in the minors, there were hecklers—players as well as fans—at every Tiger game hurling anti-Semitic epithets. According to Greenberg, the worst were the Yankees. Whenever the Tigers played the New York team, voices of hatred spewed from the Yankee dugout. True, all Jewish players, all ethnic players, suffered such baiting, but it always seemed to Greenberg and most other observers that he got more of it because he was the first Jewish superstar athlete.

Though he had learned that ignoring the harassment was the best way to handle it, this passive approach was completely against his nature. As Greenberg once told a reporter, "How the hell could you get up to home plate every day and have some son-of-a-bitch call you a Jew bastard and a kike and a sheeney without feeling the pressure?" It was tempting to respond, especially if you were the largest, most physically imposing player in the league. He did once walk over to the Yankee dugout and challenge the entire team to a fight. The entire bench looked away. But on the few occasions when he reacted with physical force, he would get thrown out of the game; then he would realize that the hecklers had won. The trick was not to respond.

Of course, there was also the tempting possibility of settling the score later, when the public was not watching. Eldon Auker, a pitcher for the Tigers, recalled an incident that happened during a game with the Chicago White Sox. Hank was running down the first base line when someone in the adjacent White Sox dugout yelled something at him—"Big yellow Jew bastard," as Auker recalled it.

Greenberg kept running to the base, and he said nothing

about the taunt for the rest of the game. There was a crowd watching and press coverage, and he had learned how to act on the field—and anyway, it was the kind of thing that happened in every game. But for some reason on this particular day, he could not live with the insult. Perhaps he had heard it too many times that week or perhaps he was just too tired. After the game, instead of his usual routine, getting a rubdown for his aching flat feet, he walked over to the White Sox clubhouse and demanded, "I want that guy who called me a yellow Jew bastard to get on his feet." None of the players spoke. They stared at their feet or a locker, avoiding his fiery gaze. Greenberg glared at each one of them, slowly turning from face to face. After a long silence, he turned around and walked back to the visitors' clubhouse.

The incident surprised Auker. "Hank rarely let it show when something was eating at him on the inside," he said. "Hank was an extremely tough guy, but he never showed that off. He wasn't one to lose his temper. He was probably the most highly respected player on the team. He was just a first-class guy, a handsome, down-to-earth gentleman." *Gentleman* is another word used regularly to describe Greenberg—along with *tough*.

The spectacle, game after game, of Greenberg the giant, stoically ignoring all the abuse hurled at him, further endeared him to American Jews and made him exactly what he didn't want to be, a Jewish hero. As Auker put it, "He just wanted to blend in." But in 1930s America, no matter how many times he said, "I just want to play baseball," neither Jews nor non-Jews were going to let him blend in. Finding a way to live with that was his struggle for most of his life. But Greenberg, in baseball and in life, always turned struggles into something positive. Four decades later, in his interview with the American Jewish Committee, Greenberg said, "You're going to have a lot of bigoted people in this world and it's not going to change, but I like to feel that being Jewish and being the object of a lot of derogatory remarks kept me on my toes all the time. . . . I could never relax and, you know, be one of the boys, so to speak. So I think it helped me in my career because it always made me aware of the fact that I had a little extra burden to bear and it made me a better ballplayer."

Whenever he encountered young Jewish players, such as Harry Eisenstat, they would ask him how to deal with anti-Semitism. His advice was always to use it to make oneself better and not as an excuse to fail. In fact, this was his advice on how to deal with any kind of adversity.

Certainly some of the attention Greenberg received was a reflection on his playing. Even though he never became a great fielding first baseman, he became the anchor of a famous double play trio. First base does not require the speed and agility of the shortstop and second baseman in this play, but it does sometimes require the ability to stretch, keeping one foot on the bag while reaching for a slightly misdirected throw. A tall man like Greenberg was well suited to that. Still, his real strength was with the bat, and his hitting was remarkably consistent. Slumps were short and rare. Many sluggers take a big swing and either hit it out of the park or strike out. Greenberg hit the home runs, but also singles, doubles, and triples. With a batting average over .300 every season for eight years in a row, from his rookie year, 1933, until he joined the army in 1941, Hank was the kind of steady hitter who could be the foundation of a winning team.

The Tigers, who had been mediocre at best for years, won the pennant in 1934, got to game seven of the World Series before they lost, and remained a contending team for the rest of the 1930s. In 1935, the year Hank broke his wrist, the Tigers won the World Series from the Cubs in six games. In 1936 Greenberg broke his wrist again in the same place at the start of the season, on April 29, in a baseline collision with the Washington Senators' Jake Powell. Greenberg was out for the rest of the season and the Tigers finished a distant second place behind the Yankees, despite 42 pitching victories between Tommy Bridges and Schoolboy Rowe. In 1937 Greenberg was back, and it was a big season for the Tigers, even though the Yankees deprived them of the pennant at the end of a hard-fought summer. And though the Most Valuable Player award for the American League went to the Tigers' Charlie Gehringer, who hit .371 that year, Greenberg regarded 1937 as his best season ever. He led the league in runs batted in, with 183, only one short of Lou Gehrig's AL record. Whether the Tigers won or lost, Greenberg often seemed to provide memorable moments, driving in runs when they were most needed, to tie the game or put his team in front in the late innings. On September 19, in a season when the Yankees seemed unstoppable with Gehrig, Joe DiMaggio, and Bill Dickey, Greenberg became the first batter ever to hit a home run into the distant center field stands in Yankee Stadium.

Success on the field was good business, too: four times between 1934 and 1940, the Tigers attracted more fans to their ballpark than any other team—some years, more than a million. And the sports world was not just watching the Tigers in the 1930s, it was watching Detroit. In 1935, the year the Tigers won their first World Series, the Detroit Lions won their first National Football League championship, and in 1936, in hockey, the Red Wings won their first Stanley Cup. One year after that, a Detroit resident, Joe Louis, won the heavyweight boxing championship. Suddenly Detroit, previously an afterthought to sports fans elsewhere, was one of the top sports cities in America.

Joe Louis rooted for the home baseball team, the Tigers, and Hank Greenberg was one of his favorite players. In July 1935 Louis came onto Navin Field in a white suit and posed with Greenberg in his baggy flannel uniform for the *Detroit*

News. The ballplayer towered over the boxer, smiling as the champ delivered a mock right jab.

The relationship between Louis and the Jews was cemented in June 1938, when Louis knocked out Max Schmeling, champion of Nazi Germany. According to the humorist Art Buchwald, who spent his early years shuttled between foster homes, boarding houses, and orphanages, one of the certainties of his childhood was that "Joe Louis was going to save us from the Nazis." The fight had been put together by Mike Jacobs, a Jew from the Lower East Side of New York and one of the leading promoters in boxing. Schmeling had previously defeated Louis, knocking him out in the twelfth round in a packed Yankee Stadium. But Louis dispatched the German in the first round in the rematch. Thus Louis was known to the Jews as the man who had defeated Hitler, although Schmeling too had a Jewish manager in the United States, Joe Jacobs, whom he refused to replace despite Hitler's demands. More important, Schmeling later proved his rejection of Nazi doctrine by hiding two Jews from a pogrom, saving their lives.

In 1938 Japan pressed its invasion of China, Germany annexed Austria, and Francisco Franco and the fascists destroyed the Spanish Republic and seized control of most of Spain. The extent of Nazi persecution of the Jews became clear in the pogrom known as *Kristallnacht*, or night of the broken glass. On that night in November 1938, the shattered windows that inspired the pogrom's name were the least of the Jews' trials. Thousands were rounded up and sent to camps, their property confiscated, and ninety-one were murdered outright. That night Schmeling was contacted by an old friend, a Jewish clothing merchant named David Lewin who feared for his fourteen- and fifteen-year-old sons, Henri and Werner. Schmeling hid the boys in his apartment in Berlin's fashionable Excelsior Hotel. The boxer informed the front desk that he was ill and did not want anyone to come to the apartment. He kept the boys hidden for several days and then helped smuggle them out of Berlin. They survived the war in Shanghai.

Meanwhile, the American public panicked in 1938 over an invasion not by fascists but by Martians. Orson Welles's Halloween radio coverage of a fictitious Martian invasion was widely taken as factual reporting. In the summer just ended, many Americans were closely watching to see whether Hank Greenberg could break Babe Ruth's record of 60 home runs in a season.

Could Hank Greenberg be the next Babe Ruth? Greenberg tried to defuse the debate. He pointed out, as he always did, that RBI were more important than home runs and that he would rather have another run at Gehrig's 184 RBI than Ruth's 60 home runs. Also, being a man of genuine humility, he categorically rejected the mantle of the next Babe Ruth. Records may fall, he noted, but Ruth was incomparable, and no one would ever measure up. The following year Greenberg wrote in an article for *Collier's* magazine, "There was only one Babe Ruth and there will never be another. Maybe Jimmy Foxx will break that record of sixty home runs. Maybe Joe Di Maggio or Rudy York or Hal Trosky or Bill Dickey will break it. Maybe I will. That won't make any of us a second Babe Ruth."

Time has proven Greenberg right. Neither Roger Maris nor Mark McGwire nor Sammy Sosa nor Barry Bonds, each of whom has beaten the 60–home run standard, has ever approached the stature of a Babe Ruth. Still, there has always been a fascination with this record, and in 1938, as Greenberg's home run count steadily rose, there was a tension, an excitement about Hank's pursuit. Greenberg, the ultimate student of batting, had become, like most batters who specialize in power, a "pull hitter." He could time the pitch so that he swung a bit early and made contact a little in front of him, which allowed him as a right-handed batter to hit the ball to left field. In his home ball field, the left field foul line was the shortest distance to a home run. This was also true of Sportsman's Park in St. Louis. The Red Sox' Fenway Park also had, and still has, a near, though very high, left field wall. Greenberg had all the American League ballparks precisely measured in his mind.

He began the 1938 season so slowly that the Tigers management began to worry about his left wrist and had it X-rayed. Greenberg declined to play in the All-Star Game, for which he was criticized, but the three days' rest made a huge difference. After the All-Star break, he started hitting home runs in bunches. In consecutive July games against the Washington Senators, he found that left field wall of Navin Field. Hank Greenberg hit two home runs in each game, and baseball aficionados figured out that the fourth homer put him ahead of where Ruth had been on that date, July 27, in his 60–home run season. Greenberg later observed the press had spent the first half of the season commenting on his slump and the second half asking if he could break Ruth's record.

Though Greenberg never wanted to encourage the press hysteria, he had in fact calculated how he might overtake the Babe. In July a New York *Daily News* reporter asked the usual question. After first laughing off the whole idea, Greenberg responded, "Seriously, though, if I can keep pace with the record until September 7, I think I can do it. Babe hit six homers that first week in September, then he tapered off. His season ended a week earlier than mine. With breaks I think I can do it."

After the first week in September, Greenberg had 46 home runs, but Ruth said he was under too much pressure to beat the record. "I don't think he'll be able to make it now," he predicted. But as Greenberg kept pace into September, Ruth changed his prediction, pointing out that late in the season pitchers get tired and pitches get easier to hit. "A great kid, Hank," said the forty-three-year-old Babe about the twenty-seven-year-old Hank Greenberg.

Though Greenberg kept insisting that he didn't care about such things, it was obvious to his teammates that he was consumed with the quest. Greenberg loved any kind of contest, and when he couldn't find one, he made one up: first one around the block, first to finish dinner. But this was a contest for the biggest record in baseball. After home run number 58, he had five games left, two in Detroit and three in Cleveland. Municipal Stadium in Cleveland was a difficult home run park, with great distances to the outfield walls, but he felt confident that he could hit two or three more home runs in Detroit before finishing the season in Cleveland.

The first of those games should have favored Greenberg. The pitcher, Howard Mills, was a left-hander, and not a particularly good one. The Tigers defeated Mills and two relievers for a 12–0 victory. But Mills kept the ball away from Greenberg, walking him twice. In three other trips, the overanxious Greenberg swung at bad pitches, striking out twice and hitting an easy pop-up. The fans booed. The next game was against the Browns' best pitcher, Bobo Newsom, trying for his 20th victory of the year. The Tigers beat him 6–2, but Greenberg never did well against the careful Newsom, and there were no home runs for the Tigers that day.

In the three games in Cleveland, Greenberg had three singles and a double, but he hit no more home runs, ending the season at 58, matching Foxx for the most to date by a hitter not named Ruth. Many Jews claimed, and still insist, that he was deliberately denied good pitches in the last five games because baseball was determined not to let a Jew beat the Babe's record. No doubt there were many people who did not want to see that record broken by a Jew. Many fans never wanted anyone to break Ruth's records. Ruth was revered. When the uncharismatic Roger Maris hit 61 home runs in the 162-game 1961 season, many fans were unhappy, and the commissioner of baseball manipulated the rules to allow Ruth to keep the record for a 154-game season. But there is no evidence of conspiracy against Greenberg. It is the job of pitchers not to give up home runs, and when a batter is hitting a lot of them, especially late in the season, a good pitcher will do all he can to get him to swing at bad pitches. If the player doesn't swing, he will walk. But at least he will not hit a home run. Sometimes the pitcher will forgo risk altogether by offering four pitches far out of the strike zone to intentionally walk the batter. These strategies were employed regularly against Greenberg—but also, routinely, against every dangerous hitter.

It would have been completely against Hank Greenberg's personal code to claim that he was denied the last three home runs because of anti-Semitism. Greenberg always thought that Mills pitched wildly because he was under so much pressure to get Hank out. In that same game against Mills, Greenberg acknowledged, Brown first baseman George McQuinn deliberately dropped a foul ball to allow Greenberg another swing, but he failed to connect on that one either.

With typical graciousness, Greenberg always insisted that he got more than his share of breaks in his run for Ruth's record. He had befriended many people in baseball, and they were rooting for him. That included some umpires. Late in the season, still on track for the record, with 56 home runs to his credit, he hit a ball to the center field wall. Flatfooted as he was, when he got to third base, the ball was still in the outfield, so Greenberg turned for home. When he slid in at the plate, the play was obscured by a thick cloud of dust, and his friend umpire Bill McGowan called him safe. McGowan stuck by the call despite the angry protest of the opposing St. Louis Browns. That was Greenberg's home run number 57. Once the season had ended, Greenberg always said that it was a bad call, and that the catcher, Sam Harshaney, had tagged him at the plate. Forty years later Harshaney wrote to Hank, wanting to straighten out the record for his college-age sons, to whom he had always insisted he had made the tag. Greenberg wrote him, "You are absolutely right. I was out by a mile and had no business being called safe. So you can tell your boys that their dad stopped Hank Greenberg from getting home run number 57."

And that, regardless of the number of home runs in the books, is who Hank Greenberg was. His mother had said that if he broke Babe Ruth's record, she would celebrate by making him 61 gefilte fish in the shape of baseballs. When the season ended with only 58 home runs, Hank smiled and said, "It's just as well. There is no way I could have eaten all that gefilte fish."

5

Henry B. Interrupted

> But to the students of most of the parochial schools,
> an inter-league baseball victory had come to take
> on only a shade less significance than a top grade
> in Talmud, for it was an unquestioned mark
> of one's Americanism, and to be counted a
> loyal American had become increasingly
> important to us during these
> last years of the war.
> —Chaim Potok, *The Chosen*

HANK GREENBERG had become one of the nation's most respected baseball players, though no one forgot that he was a *Jewish* baseball player. Jewish fans idolized him, anti-Semitic ones hurled epithets at him, as did some opposing players, and the press, which covered him constantly, seldom mentioned Greenberg without the adjective Jewish or Hebrew.

In 1940 Greenberg helped the Tigers win another pennant by batting .340, hitting 41 home runs, and driving in 150 runs. He also contributed by giving up his position at first base and moving to left field so that young Rudy York, also a great hitter, would have a place. This is often cited as proof of what a good team player Greenberg was. He didn't want to play the outfield, but he did it without complaint for the good of the team. But more telling about Hank Greenberg is the depth of his reluctance to leave first base. In one respect, first base was the absolute worst position for him to play because it meant that when the Tigers played away from Hank's fan base in Detroit, he was positioned right in front of the opposing team's dugout, which was typically along the first base line. That put him in easy earshot of anti-Semitic harassment from the home team. But he was also close enough to hurl some comments right back without being overheard by the fans. He might have welcomed a chance to escape this hot seat, but he had gotten used to it. Besides, infielders are close to the game, at the center of the action. The outfield felt "lonely." "It's like a Broadway cop being transferred to Staten Island," said Greenberg.

Though the Tigers lost the 1940 World Series in seven games to the Cincinnati Reds, it was one of Greenberg's best seasons and he seemed poised for greatness. Whether or not he broke Ruth's home run record or Gehrig's RBI record, he was certain to pile up an extraordinary number of career home runs and RBI with the playing years left to him. He was only twenty-nine years old.

But World War II had started in Europe, and though the United States was not yet directly involved, young men were required to register for the draft. It seemed likely that Greenberg was about to have his career interrupted in his prime.

For now, he was still playing championship baseball. But driving back to New York after the last game of the World Series with his brother Joe, Hank realized that this was his opportunity to register for the draft without press coverage. They chose Geneva, New York, a quiet upstate town that they happened to pass through, where registration was taking place at a local school. Joe gave the family house in Crotona Park as his address, but Hank listed his residence as the plush Detroit Leland Hotel. Greenberg always said that he didn't know why he did that. But it is not difficult to imagine. He had escaped the Bronx and was a superstar of sports, who had just experienced the excitement of a World Series. Were the war and the draft going to end all that? He might have to give up baseball, but he was not going back to the Bronx; "home" was the luxury hotel in Detroit where he stayed when he was playing baseball.

At the time it was just a small gesture. He didn't expect that there would be consequences to this decision. A hard, long season had ended, he had money in his pocket, and he was looking forward to his most lucrative contract ever. Now the best-paid player in baseball, he took the month of January off for a vacation in Hawaii. When he returned in February, flying into LaGuardia Airport, where Joe and his father were waiting to take him back to the Bronx, he was swarmed by journalists. That was how he learned that because he had registered using an address in a downtown commercial neighborhood with few qualified recruits, his number had come up early, and he was about to be drafted.

When he reported to the Detroit draft board, a doctor there examined him but found him unfit for service due to flat feet. The press immediately seized on this story. Had Greenberg used his fame and wealth to get out of military service? Some even suggested that he had bribed someone. Greenberg, who knew his sports history, recalled that heavyweight fighter Jack Dempsey was hounded for years by fans who accused him of somehow slipping out of military service in World War I, until he finally produced proof that he had been rejected on medical grounds. It became apparent to Greenberg that he needed to avoid any appearance of special treatment.

Greenberg went back for reexamination and was accepted. On May 7, 1941, only nineteen games into the season and having hit only two home runs, he was inducted into the U.S. Army. Reporters asked him how much money he was losing; he replied that after taxes it wasn't that big a loss. Hank Greenberg never got comfortable with taking bows. He would always try to say the appropriate thing, whether about the importance of Yom Kippur or about his willingness to serve his country. Invariably, he looked for a way to say, this really isn't the big thing you think it is. It was as if he were following a Talmudic injunction: "Only a fraction of a man's virtues should be enumerated in his presence."

Only a handful of major league players were drafted in 1941, and Hank Greenberg was the only big name. Morrie Arnovich would have made a better story because he had volunteered, feeling deeply his responsibility as a Jew to fight the Nazis. But Arnovich was rejected for missing molars, whose absence he tried to demonstrate with a gaping smile to reporters.

The baseball world, as if to have one last Greenberg watch, waited to see whether he would hit a home run in his last game before reporting for military service. Greenberg also wanted to go out with a homer, and he had a good chance at one because in his final game he faced Tiny Bonham and Atley Donald, neither of whom was among the Yankees' most reliable pitchers. In the bottom of the eighth, the bases were loaded with Donald on the mound. Detroit had a comfortable lead, and even some Yankee fans must have wanted to see Greenberg hit one last homer. In fact, Bill Dickey, the Yankees catcher, from his crouch behind the batter, whispered the pitches to Greenberg, assuring him he would get nothing but fastballs. But Donald threw three pitches nowhere near the strike zone.

Greenberg did not want to go out with a walk, so he started swinging—and missed, his huge powerful strokes swishing through the air. In his final at-bat before going to the army, Hank Greenberg struck out. Even his nemeses from the Yankees turned out for the farewell party that followed that game.

As Greenberg reported for duty at Fort Custer, Michigan, he did not seem worried about his future. Yes, he was losing $11,000 a month on his $55,000 contract, and he was missing most of the season. But the army was a one-year obligation, and he planned to be back in time for the 1942 season. It was not difficult duty, and he would put in his time. "I was never treated badly in the army," Greenberg said. "I minded my own business and I kept to myself a great deal. I did a lot of reading and did my army chores." In the meantime, he was a natural advertisement for army recruiting. Senator Josiah Bailey of North Carolina underestimated his salary and called him a hero for giving up $40,000 a year for just $21 a month in the military.

Greenberg spent eight months in a regular-army unit staffed by career soldiers—the Fifth Division, Second Infantry Antitank Company. They practiced laying siege to small American towns in mock battle. The two-time Most Valuable Player of the American League and star of the recent World Series was cheered by crowds as his division moved through the Midwest, including Cincinnati and Detroit, where the Series had been played only months earlier. Gone were the anti-Semitic jeers. Even anti-Semites did not jeer at a man in military uniform.

Greenberg quickly rose from private to sergeant, even though he refused to play for the company baseball team because it played on afternoons, which was time off for everyone else. Baseball looked different to a professional. It wasn't about fun. In the meantime, the draft law was changed, exempting men over the age of twenty-eight, so Greenberg, age thirty, was released early on December 5, 1941. He immediately went to Detroit and was preparing to get into shape for spring training when he heard news of the Japanese attack on the naval base in Pearl Harbor, Hawaii.

According to Jewish folklore, after safely finishing his military service, Hank Greenberg volunteered for combat because his country needed him. It was the final flourish to the Hank Greenberg legend: he sacrificed his career because he was a patriot or because he wanted to fight the Nazis. The myth was succinctly stated in a 2006 book for young readers called *Jewish Sports Stars*, whose author, David J. Goldman, asserts, "The young man who served his religion by often refusing to play ball on the High Holidays wanted to serve his country and help defeat Nazism. He could have avoided combat if he wanted to, but it was important for Hank to do his part."

Starting with the myth of his religious observance, this entire statement contains only the tiniest shards of truth. Greenberg had been discharged into the reserves, subject to recall, and, according to his own account, he reasoned that his eight-month peacetime stint was not going to satisfy his wartime draft board. If recalled, he would go back to his old unit, and he had learned enough about the military to know that he did not want to be at war in an infantry unit. Instead, he joined the Army Air Corps, where he felt that he would still be serving his country but, as he said, "in a much more pleasant way."

His military service in the Air Corps in the Pacific, predictably, was not particularly pleasant, but he was too large and possibly too old to have been a flyer, so he would not be in combat. The Air Corps was a good choice. His old antitank infantry outfit ended up attached to George Patton's Third Army in some of the bloodiest combat service in Europe, where it pushed crack German troops out of France, was among the first to cross the Rhine, battled across Germany, and linked up with the Soviets in Czechoslovakia at the war's end.

On December 9 Hank explained to the press that he was going back into the service voluntarily because of Pearl Harbor, that the attack "settles it for me." He was going in to serve his country, not necessarily to fight the Nazis, as the Jewish version would have it. The son of immigrants, he was more passionate, or at least he found it easier to express passion, for being American than for being Jewish. Typical of Greenberg, he said he was reenlisting to serve his country and to make sure he was out of the infantry, again caught between the desire to say the right thing and the impulse toward humility.

He also told the press that his baseball career was over. He had no way of knowing how long the war would last or what would happen to him. He probably thought it would be better not to perform his military service as a baseball star. But in reality, he had little choice. By now, there was no mitigating his stardom.

Dana Greenberg, a twenty-five-year-old reporter for the *Jewish News* in Detroit who was no relation to Hank, saw Hank as the unit passed through town and vividly remembered it at age ninety. "In 1942 there was a parade on November 11 and Hank Greenberg came down the street in uniform in a jeep. He stopped right in front of me. He took out a candy bar for himself and another for his buddy in the jeep. I actually saw him hand the candy bar to his buddy. It was a nice moment. It showed his character." Greenberg had become such a model of character that even his slightest gesture was singled out as a sign of greatness.

Hank Greenberg was the first active major leaguer to enlist after the Pearl Harbor attack, but three hundred minor leaguers were already in the military, and by spring training, sixty-one major leaguers had enlisted or been drafted. Eventually, five hundred major league baseball players would serve in the military in World War II. Morrie Arnovich tried again to enlist, and with the urgency of wartime, was accepted. Harry Eisenstat, wanting to fulfill his patriotic duty, quit baseball and worked in a defense plant.

Numerous players, including some of the biggest stars, like Ted Williams and Joe DiMaggio, enlisted after the 1942 season ended with the Cardinals beating the Yankees in a five-game World Series. The victorious Cardinals, in fact, lost much of their unstoppable lineup to the military. One of their star pitchers, Johnny Beazley, enlisted in the off-season, and the promising young left-hander Howie Pollet left during the 1943 season. Terry Moore and future Hall of Famer Enos Slaughter, both star outfielders, also signed up after the Series. Stan Musial, a twenty-one-year-old rookie in 1942, stayed with the Cardinals and helped them win two more pennants and another World Series before joining the navy after the 1944 season.

Moe Berg could be counted on to do something different. He worked in Europe as a spy. His knowledge of both German and physics was good enough for him to pass himself off as a German physics student and discuss the Nazi nuclear program with a top German nuclear physicist.

Major league rosters were decimated for the 1943, 1944, and 1945 seasons, most teams held together by shaky old-timers and dubious rookies. In 1944 Joe Nuxhall pitched in a game for Cincinnati at the age of fifteen. The Dodgers gave sixteen-year-old Tommy Brown, a local kid from Bensonhurst, 46 games at shortstop that year. Pete Gray played 61 games in the outfield for the St. Louis Browns in 1945 despite having lost his right arm in a childhood farm accident.

After attending officer training school in Tampa, Florida, Greenberg was stationed in Fort Worth, Texas, where he shared an apartment with the actor William Holden. Holden, seven years younger, was working on training films and had almost nothing in common with Greenberg other than being an officer in the Air Corps. Born William Beedle, Holden had grown up in southern California and came from an extremely wealthy WASP family. He had only recently become known as a movie star for his performance in *Golden Boy*, portraying a character whom Greenberg would have understood very well. Based on a play by Clifford Odets, who was born in the Bronx to Jewish immigrant parents just a few years before Greenberg, it is the story of a violinist who has an opportunity to become a prize fighter. His immigrant father is horrified at the idea that he would give up his instrument for professional boxing. It was a typical Jewish story about the athletes of Greenberg's generation. But Jews were not popular in the 1930s, so Odets, determined to write a hit and to conceal the autobiographical nature of the work, made the characters Italian.

Greenberg traveled the country as a second lieutenant, inspecting Air Corps training facilities. But he did not want to spend the entire war in the States. "Sometime in 1943," he said in his autobiography, "I decided I wasn't going to spend the rest of my military career in Fort Worth. I wanted to be assigned overseas and requested a transfer." But he was characteristically laconic about his reasons. To the press, of course, Greenberg was a patriot volunteering for combat. But while that scenario may contain an element of truth, he wasn't volunteering for combat. He wasn't trained for combat.

Although he was assigned to one of the first group of the new state-of-the-art B-29 bombers sent into combat, he didn't fly one. Instead, he was stationed first in India and then in China, traveling through war-torn Asia inspecting the operations of B-29 bomber bases. In 1945 he was sent back to New York along with combat veterans to help boost morale in defense plants. Before he left he visited a bomber base in China to see Martin Mayer, the son of his Detroit doctor. He had learned where Mayer was stationed and stopped by to ask whether there was anything Martin wanted him to relay to his father. Greenberg didn't forget people and they never forgot him.

When World War II ended there was in America a passionate desire for normalcy, and there was no better symbol of that than seeing the major leaguers come home and take to the baseball field. If Ted Williams could pound them out of Fenway Park, if Joe DiMaggio could hit them into the upper deck in Yankee Stadium, if Hank Greenberg could slam them high over the left field wall in Detroit once more, everything would be all right again. Greenberg's comeback was especially watched by fans and the press because he was one of the few players to get back early enough to play at least part of the 1945 season. Could he play the way he used to after four years away? No major leaguer had ever come back from that long an absence, but many players, sportswriters, and fans were hoping.

Getting in shape after a hiatus of more than three years was not easy, even for as methodical and obsessive a trainer as Greenberg. He was thirty-four years old: his beautiful swing looked a little slower, and his flat-footed run was even more ponderous. In his first games back, he struck out, popped up, and hit a few singles. There were a few home runs but little sign of the old Greenberg. But, as he kept reminding the press, he had always started off the season badly and he assured them that he would improve as the season went along. That first year back, he played in seventy-eight games with a batting average only two points lower than his career average of .313.

He had returned to a Tigers team in a pennant race, helping them hold off the Senators, and once again the Cubs were waiting in the World Series—for Greenberg a second chance at the matchup interrupted by a broken wrist in 1935. For Jews the sight of Hankus Pankus back slugging home runs was something to cheer about in a year of horrendous news, as details of the Holocaust were slowly becoming clearer. But the major leagues were still staffed with wartime replacements, and Greenberg, along with teammate Rudy York, stood out as one of the few first-rate players in the 1945 World Series. Acknowledging the low standards of the major leagues at the time, Greenberg described the Series as "more or less a comedy of errors."

Sportswriter Frank Graham portrayed the series played by rookies and out-of-shape newly discharged veterans as "the fat men verses the tall men at the office picnic." It was a notoriously poorly played Series. The Cub historian Warren Brown predicted that neither team could win.

The Cubs had such a limited pitching staff that they started their ace Hank Borowy in three games in eight days and brought him in as a relief pitcher in a fourth game. By game seven he was exhausted and had to be taken out of the game after giving up hits to his first three batters. Borowy was one of many ballplayers who was a star only during the war years.

Perhaps Greenberg's best moment was in game seven, when, immediately after Borowy's departure, he advanced the runners on a surprise bunt. Greenberg was a slugger, not a bunter, and no one, even on his own team, expected this. But it was not just strategy that led him to bunt. His wrist was in such pain from the previous games that a bunt was the only play he was capable of executing.

The most famous incident of the series took place off the field. Billy Sianis, owner of the Billy Goat Tavern, was asked to leave the Cubs' home stadium, Wrigley Field, because his pet goat's odor was bothering other fans. He angrily declared, "Them Cubs, they aren't gonna win no more"—an incident famously known as "the curse of the goat." The Cubs haven't been in a World Series since.

It was a tense seven-game contest, and as in 1935 the Tigers won the Series from the Cubs. Hank had driven in seven runs and hit homers in the Series, but beyond the statistics it was a thrill for Americans to see Hank Greenberg in a World Series again, with the war ended just a few months earlier.

Miraculously, of the five hundred major league players who served, many in brutal combat, only two were killed in action— Washington outfielder Elmer Gedeon and the Athletics' catcher

Harry O'Neill. Gedeon grew up in Cleveland and, like Greenberg, excelled at numerous sports. His best was track. But he turned down a spot on the U.S. Olympic track team to sign with the Washington Senators. He was drafted into an army cavalry unit in January 1941, even before Greenberg. About the time Greenberg was going in for his first stint with the infantry, Gedeon was transferred to the Army Air Corps. In February 1943 the Associated Press ran a feature story on him under the headline: "Gedeon Will Return to Baseball if War Doesn't Last Too Long." "It's a matter of time," said Gedeon. "If the war ends before I'm past the playing age I'll return to the game." But Gedeon started flying combat missions over Europe and in April 1944, while flying his thirteenth mission, he was shot down over France. His death was not confirmed until the end of the war in May 1945.

Harry O'Neill grew up in Pennsylvania and was another all-around athlete. In 1939 he had been signed by the Philadelphia Athletics with considerable excitement because of his skills and his power. At six feet, three inches, he was almost as tall as Greenberg. But the Athletics used him in only one game, against the Tigers. The Athletics were having a terrible day in Detroit on July 23, 1939, part of a terrible losing year. By the end of the fourth inning the Tigers were leading 12–1. Greenberg scored twice and drove in a run. The Athletics threw in most of their roster, nineteen players in all, and in the eighth inning they let O'Neill catch. He never got to bat and the management was insufficiently impressed with his performance to use him again. In 1942, after struggling to reignite his baseball career, he joined the Marine Corps and became a lieutenant. He was killed on March 6, 1944, fighting the Japanese on the island of Iwo Jima, shot by a sniper who, according to O'Neill's comrade, singled him out because of his height.

Gedeon and O'Neill were the only ex–big leaguers killed in the war, but they weren't the only casualties. Si Rosenthal, a

Boston Jew who played outfield for the Red Sox for two seasons in the twenties, came back wheelchair-bound for life after his mine sweeper hit a mine near Le Havre, France, in 1944. His son Buddy, serving in the Marines, was killed by Japanese fire in the Pacific in December 1945.

One of the more extraordinary stories was that of wannabe major leaguer Bert Shepard, who flew thirty-three missions in a P-38 fighter plane before being shot down. He was taken prisoner by the Germans, who amputated his damaged right leg several inches below the knee. Another captured American soldier crafted him a crude prosthetic leg. In early 1945 Shepard was freed in a prisoner-of-war exchange and sent to Walter Reed Army Medical Center in Washington, D.C., where Undersecretary of War Robert Patterson asked him what he wanted to do next. Shepard said that if he couldn't fly combat missions, he wanted to play baseball.

Patterson persuaded Clark Griffith, the owner of the Washington Senators, to arrange a tryout for Shepard. With the war still on and the teams in desperate need of players, he was signed. On August 4, 1945, days before the war ended, Shepard was called to the mound in the fourth inning of the second game of a doubleheader against the Boston Red Sox. The Senators were trailing 14–2, but Shepard struck out George "Catfish" Metkovich with the bases loaded and ended the inning. On one leg, Shepard pitched five and a third innings in his one game, giving up only one run, for an earned run average of 1.69. Since the regular players came home and he never pitched again in the majors, that day gave Shepard one of the best career ERAs in history—better, in fact, than that of the all-time career leader, Ed Walsh of the Chicago White Sox, whose mark was 1.82.

Cecil Travis, a star infielder for the Senators, returned with his feet damaged from frostbite in the Battle of the Bulge, and after two lackluster seasons, he retired midseason in 1947. The

Cardinals' Terry Moore was clearly not the player he had been before the war, his legs not allowing him to make plays he once had made in center field, his eyes and reflexes unable to cope with fastballs he used to hit. Nor could Morrie Arnovich get back his game; he drifted to the minor leagues and then retired. Other players found that they just didn't have their former concentration.

The legendary Ted Williams, who enlisted in 1942 and served as a navy pilot but was not sent overseas, was, characteristically, an exception. Seven years younger than Greenberg, when he returned to baseball in 1946, he showed little erosion of his skills. Like Greenberg, he was a great hitter, but he had a much longer career in which to amass statistics. He was also tall and handsome like Greenberg, though a more difficult personality, constantly at odds with sportswriters and fans. But he played in Boston, where both the writers and the fans get a lot rougher than in Detroit. He sardonically referred to the Boston sportswriters as "the knights of the keyboard." Williams had wit and used words well, a quality Greenberg admired. The sluggers became good friends.

Joe DiMaggio, the other slugger compared to Greenberg, was known for his lack of charm and wit. But he, too, had a friendly relationship with Greenberg. Greenberg admired DiMaggio's natural ability and thought that for all his lack of charm he had a genuineness that could be trusted. Only three years younger than Greenberg, DiMaggio came back for the 1946 season after having served in the United States as an Army Air Corps physical fitness instructor. He didn't hit with his former consistency, though, until the following season. Williams, DiMaggio, and Greenberg were the old masters of the bat. So there were many reasons to wonder what kind of ballplayer Greenberg was going to be in a postwar major league.

Not everyone was rooting for Greenberg. After the Tigers outlasted the Senators for the American League pennant,

Greenberg again heard opposing players calling him a "dirty Jew bastard." The war hadn't changed everything. Throughout the 1930s and ever since, pollsters have attempted to measure anti-Semitism in America. Those studies have shown anti-Semitism rising steadily during the 1930s and continuing to rise during World War II. For instance, a 1942 study of college-bound high school students conducted for Princeton's *Public Opinion Quarterly* asked who the respondent would not want for a roommate in college. Just 3 percent said they would not want someone who was Irish, but 45 percent said they would not want a Jew. The only less popular choice was a black roommate, with 78 percent objecting. Only 5 percent didn't care what kind of roommate they got.

But according to pollsters, anti-Semitism dropped dramatically after 1945. Some sociologists believe this stemmed from a reluctance to insult veterans and their families. Though just 4 percent of the population, Jews served in the military in disproportionate numbers, accounting for 8 percent of Americans who served in the military in World War II. Jews also accounted for almost 10 percent of American casualties, with forty thousand Jewish deaths in combat. While anti-Semitism persisted in the population, it was less common, less acceptable, and consequently less evident at baseball games than it had been before.

Greenberg was now a veteran, famous for volunteering early for combat service, and even though this was not entirely true, he was now cheered far more often than booed or taunted. He was at the height of his celebrity, and just as before the war, he counted among his friends prominent Jewish businessmen and industrialists. One such friend was Louis Marx, a Brooklyn Jew fifteen years his senior. Marx had been a manufacturer of inexpensive toys, many of which revealed a fondness for the military—toy soldiers and toy weapons. After the war, he became the largest toy manufacturer in the world.

In late 1944, before Greenberg had been discharged from

the army, Marx invited him to a lunch in Greenwich, Connecticut, at the home of his close friend and business associate Bernard Gimbel, who carried Marx's toys in his chain of department stores. There Hank met Gimbel's daughter Caral. The Gimbels, like the Marxes, were German Jews. The family had been in America since 1835 and were so assimilated that they were barely distinguishable from non-Jews. They celebrated Christmas and Easter and never went to a synagogue.

But they were Jews and they married Jews. Caral was in the throes of a divorce from her first husband, Edward Lasker. A Jewish businessman who like Caral had an interest in horses, Lasker owned and bred thoroughbreds. His father, Albert Davis Lasker, was a successful advertising executive and part owner of the Chicago Cubs. Albert Lasker is footnote in baseball history, because his proposal for a three-man commission to oversee baseball led to the creation of the post of commissioner.

Caral was pretty and wealthy, part of the acculturated, affluent world to which Greenberg had always aspired. She was athletic, a recognized equestrian champion, and she knew the sports world, though she claimed to know nothing of baseball. She told the journalist Ira Berkow that she had found Greenberg to be "the most gorgeous, handsome, virile man I had ever met." She liked his sense of humor and that though he was a superstar, he was humble and self-effacing, especially with her. When he asked her out for a first date, he gave her his telephone number in case something else turned up and she wanted to break it. She understood that this was partly insecurity because of her wealth and social standing, but there was a genuine sense of modesty that showed in everything he did. It fascinated her. Humility is part of the central mystery of Hank Greenberg. At every juncture of his life, while his qualities and accomplishments were being celebrated, Greenberg could always be counted on to punch holes in his image, calling all the praise an exaggeration. It made him different from other famous people Caral had known.

Caral was intrigued by what she saw as an attraction of opposites, an aristocrat with a sense of entitlement drawn to a man from the Bronx from an immigrant background, affluent and accomplished but still struggling for a better life. But their daughter Alva had a more nuanced view.

"She was a socialite," Alva said. "She came from a certain background, and she was spoiled. She was a nice person and a devoted friend but she was very self-centered basically. . . . [They were] an odd couple, especially since Dad was pretty self-centered too, but in a driven way. Obsessed with what he was doing. You don't get to be great if you aren't."

The distance between the Gimbels and the Greenbergs was even greater than that between Caral and Hank. The Greenbergs could not even have had a meal at the Gimbels' home, because of the Jewish dietary restrictions the Greenbergs followed. The Gimbels were old-guard German-American Jews, and the Greenbergs were from that embarrassing new wave of Yiddish speakers from the shtetl. And while Hank loved his family, he also loved that the Gimbels knew about all the things he wanted to learn about—good food and wine, fine clothes, art, design, sophistication. Hank relished the company of Bernard Gimbel, a large, athletic man who loved sports and spent a great deal of time in the company of the former heavyweight champion Gene Tunney. On many afternoons when Hank was in New York in the off season he would accompany Tunney and Gimbel to the exclusive Biltmore baths, where for the then-extravagant fee of $10 you could use the hot steam room and cold pool.

But there was an earthiness, an unpretentiousness about Hank, despite his expensive clothes, that meant that he would never fit in with Caral or the Gimbels. When he asked Caral to marry him, he acknowledged their families' differences. His proposal was awkward. "Caral, I don't believe in big weddings," he said. "Our families don't mesh. Do you want to get married or don't you?" She did. When she had married Lasker in 1935, her parents had thrown her a huge wedding, reported by the press as "one of the season's outstanding social events," but now she was delighted to get married in the living room of a justice of the peace in St. Augustine, Florida, on the way to spring training.

A serious art collector, Caral gave Hank a taste for post-Impressionists, while she took pleasure in his world of baseball. She adored Ted Williams, whom she found stunningly handsome, and could not understand why Marilyn Monroe had married a man as dull as Joe DiMaggio. When the 1946 season opened, Caral sat in a box seat in Briggs Stadium, the former Navin Field, and watched her husband hit one of his famous home runs to beat the St. Louis Browns 2–1.

But the war had changed Hank. He was thirty-five years old now, he had been too many years away from the game, and he just didn't care about it the way he once did. He still loved to get together with baseball friends like Ted Williams and talk baseball, but he now wanted more out of life. He often said that the war had completely turned him against religion, but he had never been interested in religion before the war. It is unclear how the war changed his stance or what happened during the war to change it. When friends and relatives were asked, they all said that they could not recall Hank talking of his wartime experiences. In February 1945 he did tell the *New York Times* of an incident when B-29s were taking off for a mission over Japan. Suddenly, one of the planes crashed, and Hank and the chaplain ran to the burning plane to see whether anyone could be rescued. But as they approached the flaming wreck, a bomb went off, knocking both of them into a nearby rice paddy while red hot metal shards shot through the air. Greenberg was knocked out and could not speak or hear for several days. Miraculously, not a single crewmember was killed. But Greenberg told the *Times'* Arthur Daley, "That also was an occasion, I can assure you, when I didn't wonder whether or not I'd be able to return to baseball. I was quite satisfied just to be alive."

Being married had changed him too. He could no longer remain totally dedicated to the game of his childhood. He had been out of the Bronx for more than fifteen years now, and neither the baseball life nor the players held the same fascination they once had. Like most of the other players, he had stayed single and had brief romances, none of them very serious. Long before Marx took him to the Gimbels', Jewish friends were constantly trying to fix him up with Jewish girls. But baseball had been a bachelors' game, and before Caral, Hank had not been looking for a serious involvement. Ballplayers lived in hotels, traveled a great deal, spent long hours at the ballpark. Marriage was not part of the culture of professional baseball, and when a player got married it was time for him to think about moving on to a different life.

Hank's hitting performance was still good by most measures, but not up to the standard of the legendary Hank Greenberg. After he was passed over for the midseason All-Star Game, there were rumors that he was planning to retire. It was even suggested that he might be going into his in-laws' department store business. Hank told the press that he was disappointed because he had wanted his wife to see him in an All-Star Game, but that would not make him quit. He called that "baby stuff," but did admit to the *New York Sun*, "I'm playing so badly I ought to quit." He acknowledged that he was not the hitter he once was, and talked about the game not being fun anymore.

By now the Tigers had traded Rudy York and needed Greenberg back on first, but older and a step or two slower, he didn't have command of the position anymore. Balls were getting by him that shouldn't have, and since it was widely known that he was one of the highest-paid players in baseball, more was expected of him. The same Detroit fans who had loved him when he returned from the war were booing him now. The joy had gone out of the game for him.

But late in the summer, in typical Greenberg fashion, he managed to turn things around. He started hitting home runs again, and by September, he was second only to Ted Williams in the American League in home runs for the season. By the end of the season he had beaten Williams, 44 homers to 38, and he also drove in the most runs, 127 to Williams's 123. Still, it was the first full season in his major league career with a batting average under .300. And with 15 errors, this had been one of his worst seasons defensively.

When the season was over, he went back to New York to settle happily into married life in a large apartment on the affluent Upper East Side of Manhattan. Not long after Caral had their first child, a son named Glenn, he received a telegram from Billy Evans, the general manager of the Tigers:

> This is to inform you that your contract has been assigned to the Pittsburgh club of the National League. Trust you will find your new connection a most profitable one.

This was a bitter blow. Greenberg had spent his entire twelve-year career in the Detroit organization, and now they didn't even trade him. Instead they let a low-standing team take over his contract for a mere $10,000. The maneuver is what baseball does to over-the-hill superstars to free up money to buy young talent. The Yankees hadn't treated Babe Ruth any better. In 1934 they had sent him away from the "house that Ruth built" to the Boston Braves. The Braves tried to make the deal look better by giving him stock and saying he was a part owner, but the organization was bankrupt and the stock worthless. Greenberg, who greatly admired Ruth, had always been troubled by the way baseball had treated him.

The Pittsburgh Pirates had finished the 1946 season in

seventh place. Only the once-great New York Giants, the team that Greenberg had followed as a boy, ranked lower in the National League. By sending him to a National League team, the Tigers made sure that Greenberg would not be hitting against them. Ironically, the Dreyfuss family, which had owned the Pirates since the nineteenth century, had recently sold the team, which was thus under non-Jewish ownership for the first time in sixty years.

Greenberg showed his Tiger contract to business friends in Detroit, but they told him that since he had signed it, there was nothing to be done. Since the early days of baseball, contracts included a "reserve clause," which meant that players signed for one year and then the club had the right to renew the contract unilaterally for as little as 80 percent of the previous year's salary. Players had no negotiating leverage because they were not allowed to offer their services to another team. But the club had the right to trade or sell the player to another team whenever it pleased.

Hank, Caral, and Glenn moved to Pittsburgh to an apartment Caral found depressing. It was far from the Upper East Side. Meanwhile, Greenberg had negotiated a pioneering deal with Pittsburgh that showed his business savvy. First, he got out of the reserve clause, a unique maneuver at the time, agreeing only to a one-year nonrenewable contract. The financial terms he worked out were complicated, with a base salary and shares in the club to be sold back at the end of the season at a higher price, and with the capital gains tax covered. The exact value of the deal was never released to the press, but many believe that this was the first time a baseball player earned in one season more than $80,000, which was Babe Ruth's top salary. In fact, some believe that this was the first time a player broke the $100,000 mark. While most players were easily exploited, Greenberg was shrewder and more effective than most modern agents. He speculated that the Tigers had sold him because they were tired of his negotiations. It occurred to him that their irritation with his business skills might have included a touch of anti-Semitism.

Greenberg's season in Pittsburgh was not a memorable one for the Pirates or for the player. He ended the season with the lowest batting average of his career, with the fewest home runs and runs batted in of any full season, and his fielding skills were at their worst. At one point, he got into a locker room brawl with a teammate, pitcher Jim Bagby, because a batter had hit an easy ball to first base and Greenberg had missed it. Bagby called him "a big Jew son of a bitch" and said that for the money he was making he should be able to catch a ball like that. Greenberg told Bagby, a six-foot-two second-generation major leaguer, that he was going to get him after the game. The two had known each other before the war, when they were both in their prime and in better frames of mind. According to a story told by Ted Williams, the first time Greenberg ever saw Williams bat was when the Red Sox were playing in Detroit in 1939. Greenberg was leaning forward at first base anticipating a weak pop-up or grounder from the rookie. But Bagby, having witnessed what the new kid could do, shouted from the Red Sox bench, warning Greenberg not to play close. Greenberg was not going to listen to the opposing pitcher, and he held his ground. Bagby, who took a lot of teasing because of a speech impediment caused by a cleft palate, finally shouted to Greenberg, "All right, Hank, if you want to look like me and talk like me, stand right where you are."

That was eight years earlier, when both players were at the top of their game. Now they were both playing badly and frustrated. Bagby was angry because a good first baseman is essential to a winning pitcher, and while he was not pitching well, he was also being hurt by Greenberg's bad fielding. After the game Bagby was first into the tiled-floor clubhouse and changed out of his spikes. Greenberg had not forgotten Bagby's anti-Semitic remark, but as he charged into the clubhouse, his spikes slipped on the floor, and Bagby was able to give him a black eye before teammates held the two back.

Although Bagby had called him "a big Jew son of a bitch," Greenberg usually ignored such language. The problem was that Bagby had been right about the hit. It was one that any major league first baseman should have been able to handle.

When the Pirates acquired Hank Greenberg, they moved the left field wall in thirty feet because that was where Greenberg liked to hit home runs. The new seating was called "Greenberg Gardens." But Hank's teammate Ralph Kiner, in only his second year in the majors, was finding those seats more often than the old pro. Before long, Greenberg Gardens became "Kiner's Korner." This inevitable cycle—the fading star being replaced by the new kid on the team—was exactly why old veterans snubbed rookies. But Greenberg was different. He coached and advised the younger player, whose talents he recognized.

Growing up in Los Angeles in the 1930s, Kiner had idolized Hank Greenberg. So it was the fulfillment of a dream when, in their first spring training together, instead of turning a cold shoulder, Greenberg invited the rookie to take some batting practice with him. Soon it became a habit for Greenberg and Kiner to take extra practice at home and at away games. Hank taught Kiner to stand close to the plate and pull the ball to left. He also taught him how to steal signs from the catcher when he was on base and Greenberg at bat. Kiner could then signal to Greenberg what the upcoming pitch was. And Hank taught the youngster to deliberately mis-swing at a certain pitch early in the game; later, in a decisive situation, the pitcher might give him the same pitch again, and he could slam it. Greenberg even taught the younger man to dress well. Kiner went on to become, like Greenberg, one of the great right-handed pull hitters of all time—and eventually, like Greenberg, a Hall of Famer. The two became lifelong friends, one of Greenberg's few enduring baseball friendships. In later years, Ralph Kiner called Greenberg "the biggest influence in my life."

In the 1947 season the focus was not on Hank Greenberg but on the breach of the "color line" by Jackie Robinson and the Brooklyn Dodgers. Though a few African American players had played in the major and minor leagues in baseball's early days, a racist wall soon was constructed around the game. In an infamous incident in 1883, Cap Anson, one of the star players of his day, refused to let his Chicago White Stockings take the field for an exhibition game against the Toledo Blue Stockings, whose catcher was Moses Fleetwood Walker, an educated man who was to be the first black major leaguer. Anson ultimately had to play or forfeit his earnings, but on two later occasions he succeeded in having Walker and another African American star kept off the field. After Walker and his brother Welday played a season in the American Association, then a major league, owners established the unwritten "gentleman's agreement" that black players would not be allowed in big league baseball. Some minor leagues made the ban explicit, and by the end of the nineteenth century, there was no place for blacks in organized baseball. In 1939, when the Baseball Hall of Fame decided to induct nineteenth-century stars, Cap Anson was among the first to be honored.

But by the 1940s race relations were changing. The military was becoming integrated, there was a nascent civil rights movement, and some of the best players in baseball were in the Negro Leagues, a wealth of talent waiting for the team with the courage to tap it. In 1945 Branch Rickey, the Brooklyn Dodgers' general manager, signed Jackie Robinson, an all-around athlete and a talented twenty-six-year-old infielder. Rickey sent him to

Montreal in the Class AAA International League in 1946 and brought him up to the Dodgers in 1947.

At his first meeting with Robinson, in 1945, Rickey told him, "I'm looking for a ballplayer with guts enough not to fight back." Rickey obviously had reached the same conclusion as Greenberg, that the only way to deal with the haters and bigoted baiters on the ball field was to ignore them and show them up by digging in and trying harder. Rickey never said that he had learned his approach from Hank Greenberg, but before Jackie Robinson, Hank was the most prominent example of a ballplayer facing bigotry.

Jackie Robinson was even more abused than Hank Greenberg. Racist epithets were hurled at him by spectators and players at every at-bat, every play, every time he set foot on a baseball diamond. He even received death threats. The Phillies, spurred on by their manager, Ben Chapman, were particularly vicious. When the New York Yankees had been abusive to Hank Greenberg, one of the ringleaders had been an outfielder—the same Ben Chapman. When the Dodgers played the Phillies, several players reminded Robinson of the death threats leveled against him by pointing bats at him and pretending they were machine guns. Some players, in the spirit of Cap Anson, said they would refuse to play against the Dodgers if Robinson took the field. Even a number of Dodgers, especially the southerners on the roster, rebelled against management when Robinson joined the team. When they threatened a boycott, Rickey called their bluff, trading the South Carolina–born pitcher Kirby Higbe to the Pirates.

Greenberg understood how it would work, knew that battling victimization can make you better. In an interview with the *Daily News* he predicted, "The more they ride him the more they will spur him on. It threw me a lot when I first came up. I know how he feels." Greenberg was right. Robinson took the abuse stoically, even though he was not stoic by nature—he had a history, even in the military, of defiance in the face of racism. But he endured, mostly in silence, because that was the deal he had made with the Dodger organization. Robinson was a skilled player, but there were better and more experienced black players. He was picked to be first because he seemed to have, like Hank Greenberg, remarkable strength of character.

In May the Dodgers played the Pirates. There were tensions because some of the Pirates admired Robinson and others—Robinson's former teammate Higbe, for example—were violently opposed to the whole idea that a black man would play on a major league team. Robinson always had problems with pitchers. "Bean the black guy" was an almost reflex approach for some during the first decade of major league integration. In the 1930s, beaning the Jew had been standard practice.

When the Dodgers came to town, Pirate manager Billy Herman instructed his pitchers that if Robinson ever got to a 3-balls, no-strikes count, they should just send him to first by hitting him hard with the next pitch. In the first game of the series, the Pirate pitcher fired a ball at Robinson, forcing him to dive to the ground to avoid being hit. Some of his teammates shouted angrily at the pitcher, which was a gratifying moment for the black rookie. In the second game, Higbe threw a fastball at Pee Wee Reese's head. He had remembered his fellow southerner Reese as one of the early Robinson supporters on the Dodgers. Reese got up and on the next pitch hit a home run.

Hank Greenberg recalled in his autobiography, "Jackie paid them no mind. He got on the bases and started dancing. It was beautiful to watch. I couldn't help but admire him." Greenberg thought Robinson endured far more than he ever had. "Jackie had it tough," Greenberg said. "Tougher than any ballplayer who ever lived." But he saw in Robinson a man who was perfecting the ideal he himself had struggled toward. "He was like a prince," Greenberg said. "He kept his chin up and kept playing as hard as he could."

In the Dodgers' first game against the Pirates, Greenberg drew a walk. Robinson was playing first base for Brooklyn, so there they were together, the black man and the Jew—according to pollsters, the last choice for college roommate and the second to last. They chatted. The press later asked Robinson about the conversation and he quoted the veteran's advice: "Stick in there. You're doing fine. Keep your chin up." Then he added his own view of Hank Greenberg, "Class tells," Robinson said. "It sticks out all over Mr. Greenberg."

Sometimes it is easier to gain perspective from observing other people's experience than when you're participating in your own. Seeing Jackie Robinson's struggle threw Hank's own experience into sharp relief. Watching his own losing team harassing Robinson, Greenberg reconfirmed what he already knew about bigots, that they were stupid, backward people not worthy of a reply. He wrote in his autobiography, "I got to thinking, here were our guys, a bunch of ignorant, stupid Southerners who couldn't speak properly, who hadn't graduated from school, and all they could do was make jokes about Jackie. They couldn't recognize that they had a special person in front of them, a gem. They just kept ragging him and calling him names." It was the final piece in a puzzle he had been working out for twenty years. As a young player he had taken on bigots in plain view of the crowds. Then he learned to do it more discreetly in the clubhouse. But that hadn't really worked either. Watching Robinson, he could see that the best course was not to take them on at all, that they simply were not worth engaging with in any way.

Hank Greenberg retired from baseball at the end of the 1947 season. Largely coincidence, there is nevertheless a perfect symmetry to Greenberg's last year being Robinson's first. By now, blacks had replaced Jews on the frontline of American racism. Even fascist-leaning Detroiters had switched their target. In 1942, twenty-six thousand white workers at Detroit's Packard plant had walked off the job to protest the promotion of three black workers, and one shouted into a microphone that he would rather see Adolf Hitler win the war than "work beside a nigger on the assembly line."

Like many Jews of his generation, Hank Greenberg never forgot his experiences with anti-Semitism and did not hesitate to speak out against racism. Then, too, there was the lesson of Ben Chapman, that blacks and Jews often had the same enemies. When Jackie Robinson retired, nine years after his own retirement as a player, Hank Greenberg sent him a letter.

> Dear Jackie
>
> Having had the privilege of watching you break in to major league baseball and having observed your long and illustrious career as an active player, I want to express to you my admiration for the exemplary manner in which you have conducted yourself—both on and off the field.
>
> In my opinion you have been a credit to baseball and an inspiration to thousands of other youngsters, who will attempt to emulate your example.
>
> Sincerely,
> "Hank" Greenberg

Hank connected with Jackie Robinson only one other time. In 1970 a black player, Curt Flood, after a distinguished twelve years as an outfielder for the St. Louis Cardinals, was traded to the notoriously racist Philadelphia Phillies. The Phillies had given Robinson some of his worst encounters with bigotry, and Flood, a civil rights activist who had marched in the South, refused to go. This led to a famous court case against the reserve clause, the clause in a player's contract that let his team completely control his career. The case ultimately went to the Supreme Court. Former Supreme Court Justice Arthur Goldberg, the last of eleven children of Ukrainian immigrants, argued for Flood—the old alliance of blacks and Jews. Both Robinson and Greenberg testified on Flood's behalf against the reserve clause. Greenberg and his friend and partner Bill Veeck, with whom by then he had spent more years as a general manager and co-owner than he had spent as a player, were the only representatives of baseball management who testified for Flood.

6

Escaped at Last

Child labor! The child must carry
His fathers on his back.
—Delmore Schwartz, "The Ballad
of the Children of the Czar"

GREENBERG HAD signed a one-year contract with the Pirates and announced his intention to retire at the end of the
season. It had been a losing season though Greenberg, despite
a batting average of .249, his lowest since he played for Hartford in 1930, had delivered exactly on his promise when he had
signed to hit 25 home runs. Hank was later amused to recall
that the team wanted to lose its final game to secure last place
behind the Phillies, which would put them in line for the first
draft pick the following year. Instead they won, tied for last
place, and lost a coin toss for the first draft pick. He laughed,
"The other 153 games that we tried to win, most of them we

lost." But between Hank Greenberg's fading star and Ralph Kiner's rising one, the team had a record attendance that losing season, drawing more than a million fans for the first time.

Though he had friends such as Kiner on the team, it was a losing team and he was used to teams that won. He did not enjoy the company of many of his teammates, especially the ones who had jeered at Robinson. He was in a town he didn't know, one that his wife disliked. The longtime lover of racket ball sports had developed debilitating bone chips in one arm from playing squash. But more than anything, he had lost his passion for baseball. He said in his autobiography, "I decided that there must be other important things in life besides baseball. In the service my horizons were expanded. Then after the war I met Caral and was enthralled by her. Suddenly other places and things seemed important to me and my interest in baseball, which had been all-consuming up until then, began to wane." To many baseball players retirement is a dreaded door to an uncertain future, but in 1947 Hank Greenberg was looking forward to a new life. He saw a destiny beyond baseball.

As he approached the age of forty, Hank, now frequently Henry B. Greenberg, started to feel that he was becoming the man he wanted to be. He had married into the American-Jewish aristocracy and he dressed the part. Greenberg's daughter, Alva, said of her father, "He was a guy who was somehow sophisticated. Long before he met my mother. He had the top hat. He had the looks, the Hollywood stance, the wardrobe. An impeccably dressed guy—always. Expensive clothes. Handkerchief in the pocket. Beautifully decked out. Well shaven. Well groomed. That didn't happen when he met my mother. That happened way before."

Yet style didn't equal extravagance in his case. He was a careful money manager who declared in his autobiography that he retired from baseball with $300,000, mostly in treasury and war bonds—a remarkable achievement for a man whose total major league income, according to his calculations, was $447,000.

He was living the life. Caral was a serious art collector and he had acquired a taste for collecting too—a few small Impressionist paintings, a Gauguin that she gave him. He had become a voracious reader and loved the historical novels of James Michener. He also read everything he could find about World War II and the Nazis, fascinated that something so cultish and strange and cruel actually took place in his lifetime.

He was happy that he had left the Bronx, happy he had not gone into the garment business like his brothers. In his 1980 interview with the American Jewish Committee, Greenberg talked about baseball saving him from his siblings' fate. "The thing it did for me is [it] taught me to live in a world outside of a Jewish world. My brothers and sister, their whole life is in the Jewish society. They live in a neighborhood where there are predominantly Jews, they go to school where most of the students are Jewish, their social life is all wrapped up among Jews. My whole life was wrapped up among Gentiles."

Of course, there were many Jews in his world, but there was no Jewish observance and no Jewish education for his two sons and his daughter. Ironically, that day in 1934 when he went to a Detroit synagogue rather than play baseball remained the only Yom Kippur he ever observed as an adult. He placed no value on a Jewish education that taught him to read Hebrew without understanding the words. "All the years I was going to synagogue I didn't know what I was reading. . . . It meant nothing to me." He simply did not like religion or religious practice. "I think religion has caused more animosity and hatred among people than anything else," he said. "I think the Jews are just as bad as any other religion. . . . I think that if the Jewish race were the majority we'd have the same problems that we have today."

When the American Jewish Committee questioned him about his Jewish identity, he seemed lost, as though he didn't

understand the question. Finally he said, "When you're a minority you're automatically aware of being a minority." And
that was the extent of his Jewish identity. He accused the inter-
viewer of trying "to get me to say that there is something special about being a Jew. Isn't it just an accident of birth?"

This phrase, "accident of birth," was not unusual among the
Jews of the World War II generation. In his 1948 novel *The
Naked and the Dead*, Norman Mailer uses that exact phrase to describe a Jewish character's feelings about being Jewish. Implicit
is the shocking realization that the Nazis actually murdered six
million people simply because of that accident of their birth.

Bill Veeck, one of the more colorful men in the history of
baseball, was determined to keep Greenberg connected to the
sport. Veeck was a man of high principles, like Greenberg, but
also of crass showmanship. His principled side was very much
like Greenberg. His showman side was the complete opposite.
The exploding scoreboard packed with fireworks to punctuate
home runs and other dramatic moments was only one of the
many Veeck inventions.

Veeck insisted that even a losing team could draw fans and
make money if its management made the ballpark experience
fun. "You can draw more people with a losing team, plus bread
and circuses," he would say, "than with a losing team and a
long, still silence." His most famous stunt was staged in August
1951, when he owned the St. Louis Browns. Veeck had approached a three-foot-seven-inch-tall midget in Chicago,
Eddie Gaedel, a man in his mid-twenties, and asked him,
"Eddie, how would you like to be a big league ballplayer?"

Bill Veeck had grown up in baseball. His father had been
president of the Cubs and a good friend of the Giants' longtime
manager John McGraw. Veeck always insisted that the idea for
Gaedel came not from James Thurber's short story about a
midget sent up to bat, "You Could Look It Up," but from

McGraw. Because the strike zone, the area through which a pitch must pass or be counted a ball, depends in part on the distance between the batter's shoulders and his knees, a midget would have a much smaller strike zone than the usual player. This zone, according to the rule book, is measured according to the batter's "natural stance." Since Gaedel had never before been to bat in the major leagues, Veeck decided that any stance Gaedel took must be considered natural. So Veeck instructed him to stand in a deep crouch; according to Veeck's calculations, Gaedel's strike zone was one and a half inches from top to bottom, smaller than the two-and-three-quarter-inch diameter of a baseball. Therefore, it would be nearly impossible to throw Gaedel a strike. Then Veeck ordered him not to swing at any pitch.

Veeck paid Gaedel $100 for the day and gave him a uniform with the number 1/8. When the midget came to the plate as a pinch hitter, even the pitcher could barely contain his laughter. Gaedel walked on four pitches, then was replaced by a pinch runner at first base. The fans loved it. The lords of baseball did not, and that was the end of Gaedel's big league career.

In 1946, Bill Veeck bought the Cleveland Indians—unlike those later Browns, a team with some promising players. The following year, when he learned of Greenberg's imminent retirement, he fastened on the idea of bringing Hank into his organization in some way. At this point, no one else was pursuing Greenberg because he had made his intention to retire well known. Besides, he was no longer considered worth his high salary as a player. Veeck claimed Greenberg from Pittsburgh for the one-dollar waiver price, a claim that went unchallenged by any other team. "I felt that baseball would be foolish to let a man of Henry's class and intelligence and background get away," Veeck wrote in his memoirs.

Veeck hoped that while Greenberg was learning the business side of baseball, he would also be a part-time player for the

Indians. They met in New York in October 1947 after game seven of one of the great New York World Series, in which the Yankees came from behind and beat the Dodgers 5–2. But Greenberg made it clear to Veeck that he had no interest in playing anymore and, in fact, was looking forward to leaving baseball entirely. He and Caral were about to go out west on vacation to pursue his new athletic passion, tennis. Starting with the tennis courts in Crotona Park, and handball and squash at the 92nd Street Y, tennis and its variations had long been his off-season sports and fitness regimen. Now he was on a permanent off-season and free to play tennis every day with his athletic wife.

But Veeck was undeterred. He followed the Greenbergs to Phoenix and told Hank that he was wasting himself on the tennis court, that he belonged in baseball. To Caral's relief, Hank was not persuaded, even by the persuasive Veeck, and they moved on to more tennis in California. Once again, Veeck caught up with them. This time, he talked Hank into joining the business end of the club, and Hank and Caral moved to Cleveland.

Veeck and Greenberg had a great deal in common, despite their different origins, and they remained close friends all their lives. Both were World War II veterans; Veeck, in fact, had had a leg amputated after an injury from an antitank gun accident during the war. The men shared a sense of humor as well. Veeck's second wife, Mary Frances, recalled that the two were "always joking. Told great stories together. When Hank told a story he could never finish because he would break up laughing. 'Stop laughing. We can't hear the story,' we would say."

More profoundly, both men liked to champion the underdog, as their support of Curt Flood against the mainstream of baseball management demonstrates. Veeck, in fact, had wanted to integrate the major leagues even before Jackie Robinson joined the Dodgers. In 1942, when the Phillies were up for sale, he planned to buy them and build a winning team by staffing the club with top Negro Leagues players. According to Veeck, the plan went awry when he mentioned the idea to Commissioner Landis, an old friend of the family—Veeck's father had been one of the owners who made Landis the first commissioner—and Landis arranged for someone else to buy the team.

Veeck, with Greenberg, did integrate the American League, just eleven weeks after the National League Dodgers' Jackie Robinson, when he signed outfielder Larry Doby from the Negro National League. Veeck later claimed that he received twenty thousand angry and often threatening letters about signing a black player. A year later he signed Satchel Paige, who may have been the greatest pitcher of all time, though the color line had robbed major league fans of a chance to see him in his prime. Paige was lean and almost as tall as Greenberg, with enormous feet and a casual saunter to the mound that filled the fans with excitement. No one knew his age, but he was at least in his early forties and possibly considerably older when Veeck signed him. Partly through their willingness to create an integrated team, Veeck and Greenberg built a championship club. After winning one of the tightest pennant races in the history of the American League, the Indians went on to beat the Boston Braves in the World Series in six games, four of them decided by one or two runs. Nineteen forty-eight had been the best season in Cleveland Indian history.

Veeck and Greenberg had been partners in a grand plan to integrate baseball. While Veeck, the general manager and part owner, signed top Negro Leagues players, Greenberg, also a part owner, directed the farm system and signed many young black players. In the early 1950s, as major league teams were finally starting to acquire black players, Greenberg signed more than anyone else in baseball. Veeck sold his interest in the Indians in 1949, divorced, remarried, and in 1951 bought 80 percent of the St. Louis Browns. Greenberg stayed on in

Cleveland, where he had settled with Caral and their two sons. In 1952 their daughter, Alva, was born. The children speak fondly of their Cleveland childhood, the years when the family was together and happy. Caral had her horses, was involved with the Cleveland Museum, and had season tickets to the famous Cleveland Orchestra. She enjoyed her life in Cleveland, a very different life from Hank's.

The Indians did not win a World Series after 1948, but they did win an American League–record 111 games to take the pennant in 1954, before being swept in four games by the Giants in the World Series. After that the Indians' record began a long decline. Greenberg had a reputation as a somewhat volatile general manager who did not get along well with owners or players, in sharp contrast to his popularity as a player. Of course, he had always been a tough money negotiator, and moving to the management side of the table didn't change that. Al Rosen, a young Jewish star, never forgave Greenberg for refusing his money demands. And in 1954, at least according to legend, Greenberg lost rookie Venezuelan shortstop Luis Aparicio to the Chicago White Sox in a fight over a signing bonus. Aparicio went on to have a Hall of Fame career. In 1957, after his fellow owners backed out at the last moment from a move to Minneapolis that he had carefully negotiated, Greenberg stepped down as general manager and sold his shares in the club. There is some question about whether he was fired or quit in anger, but in any event he left Cleveland and moved back to New York.

Greenberg's self-assessment as a player in his autobiography seems to apply equally to Greenberg the front-office man. "Looking back," he said, "I guess I was tough to handle. I played hard, tried my best, I was always trying to overachieve."

Veeck's first wife, Eleanor, was an equestrian like Caral. But in time both marriages ended, and each man remarried. Both

Caral and Hank said that the cultural difference between them was too far to bridge. For all of Hank's love of the elegant life, he was too down to earth for the world of the Gimbels. He had his baseball team and she had her horses and her friends in the art world. He didn't even like the horses, and Caral said that when he got on one he looked frightened. Essentially, they lived different lives. Even the fact that she slept late in the morning became divisive, because that was not how he was raised. Mary Frances Veeck, Bill's new wife, said, "The problem with Hank and Caral was that she didn't know anything about baseball life. He would try to do her things but he loved baseball. He loved it when Toots Shor said, 'Hiya bum.'"

Finally it was Caral who asked for the divorce, in 1958, a bitter blow for Hank, who tried to talk her out of it for the sake of their children. Glenn was now twelve, Steve ten, Alva seven. Yet he was the classic workaholic parent, leaving early, coming home late, struggling to find any time for his family. He had focused what little time he spared on his firstborn, Glenn, and at the time of the divorce admitted sadly that he had never really gotten to know Steve. Alva, the girl, was a bit of a mystery to Hank. She always felt that she had the good fortune of lower expectations and therefore little pressure from her father. Hank and Caral fought over the children and eventually settled on joint custody.

The following year Veeck and Greenberg became partners again, buying control of the Chicago White Sox. The partnership seemed a great success. Their first season the White Sox won the American League pennant for the first time since 1919, when eight of their players had been accused of throwing the World Series in the biggest scandal in baseball history. Veeck and Greenberg had brought the White Sox back. But in 1961 Veeck sold his shares, and soon after Greenberg did the same.

The American League planned to add a new team in Los Angeles and wanted Greenberg to be its owner. Greenberg said that he would sign on only in partnership with Veeck. But a tremendous fight broke out with the Dodgers, who had moved to Los Angeles in 1958 and did not want Veeck, the premier promoter, in their town with a competing team. Without Veeck, the Greenberg deal collapsed. The new team, the Angels, started play in 1961 despite the Dodgers' objections.

Greenberg was never comfortable with other club owners. He was the kind of businessman who thought a handshake was as good as a contract. He didn't like the insincere and untrustworthy way owners dealt with players. Veeck was the one exception. Few of the other owners at the time seemed interested in Greenberg's ideas for baseball, such as regular-season games between National and American League teams, an idea that was finally embraced decades later. Veeck had had more success. He championed the idea of a designated hitter, a skilled batter who would go to the plate in place of the pitcher. This was an ideal job for an older player who still had his hitting skills but had lost a step defensively. Veeck always believed that if the designated hitter had been part of the game in the 1940s, the Tigers might have kept Greenberg on, and he would have remained a player a few years longer. As it turned out, the first designated hitter, Ron Blomberg of the Yankees, was Jewish.

Veeck got back into the game, purchasing the White Sox again in 1975, and Greenberg briefly became a quiet minority partner. He and Veeck remained close friends, and Hank would send Mary Frances caviar in what she termed "big, vulgar amounts." Veeck and Eleanor had three children, and he and Mary Frances had six more. The numerous Veeck children would delight in visits with the huge ballplayer. They liked to play "Gulliver," a game in which Greenberg was the giant and lay stretched out on the floor as the Lilliputian Veecks climbed over him and tied him up. When he could find the time, Hank liked to play.

Hank Greenberg's days in baseball really had ended in 1961, when, as a divorced man with three children, he moved back to New York. There, his fashionable Upper East Side apartment contained more artwork than baseball memorabilia, and he did not talk a great deal about the sport. According to Alva, his apartment looked very much like the one nearby that he had shared with Caral. It was even designed by the same fashionable decorators, Denning and Fourcade, whom Alva described as "the preeminent decorating duo of that time." Her father, she said, was "a man of humble beginnings, but he picked it all up pretty quickly. He lived in a very beautiful town house."

Greenberg settled into his New York life. He renewed his friendship with Louis Marx, the toy manufacturer, and his younger brother David. David had been pushed to the background in the toy business because Louis was an extremely aggressive and capable businessman. But Greenberg noticed that David was a highly intelligent man with a strong interest in the stock market. Greenberg had been increasingly interested in the market as well, and they soon formed a partnership, MG Securities, a company whose only purpose was to manage their investments. They had a Midtown office with a stock ticker. Alva remembered the office on Fifth Avenue at 53rd Street. "The ticker tape would be running. Quite an impressive spread. He had a secretary at one point. His days were full of the stock market. Watching his investments. Then he'd play tennis and have lunch and play backgammon. Then he'd read. He had a very nice life. He was a very smart man. I think he was just interested in too many things intellectually to be pining away for baseball."

He struggled to find time to be with his children without fans intruding. When he tried to take them to ballgames, he would be swarmed by admirers and would leave halfway through the game. The same thing could happen at a steak house. By this time he was accustomed to being pursued by fans. He tried to be gracious, but sometimes they tried his patience. According to Caral, he could be generous and kind to fans, but occasionally, especially if he was trying to do something with his family, he would show his irritation.

Hank seldom went to Old Timers Day games, saying it depressed him to see the other players looking older and older. He saw DiMaggio on occasion and Ralph Kiner, and sometimes he played tennis with Ted Williams. He perfected his tennis game with the same methodical determination he had used in baseball, playing every day, studying his swing. Bernard Karlin, a Brooklyn-born tennis instructor, played against Greenberg in the Catskills in the 1970s, when Greenberg was in his sixties. According to Karlin, "He was an aggressive player, he loved to play the net, even over the net. Not a backcourt player. He didn't have much style but he had great hand-eye coordination. He was affable, but when the ball was in play he was very active. He went across the net and he poached a lot"—cut off the ball before it could reach his backcourt doubles teammate. "He was a very effective doubles player. You could tell he had been an athlete. And he played to win."

Hank's three children, descended on both sides from famous Jews, had little awareness of a Jewish identity. When they moved to New York, Hank made an effort to reconnect with his family, having seen little of them since his marriage. Those visits with Sarah and David were his children's first encounters with traditional Judaism. One night Hank told his children, "My family is coming over for dinner tonight." When David and Sarah arrived, they started passing out books. And David put on a yarmulke. The children did not know what was happening, but they were about to experience their first Passover seder.

After the divorce Glenn and Steve were staying with their father and Alva was a few blocks away with her mother. One morning Hank woke up the two boys, saying, "Get dressed but I'm not taking you to school. We are going someplace special today."

"Why?" the boys wanted to know. Hank said, "This is Yom Kippur. That's the holiest day of the year for Jews."

The boys got dressed in jackets and ties. But instead of taking them to a synagogue, Hank took them to the planetarium at the Museum of Natural History to gaze at the stars. According to his son Steve, after about a half hour of studying the sparkling constellations projected above them, Greenberg said, "Okay, boys. That's good." And he took them to lunch to celebrate the fasting day.

Steve liked to joke that he grew up thinking Yom Kippur was the day the Jews went to the planetarium. "But what I came to realize," Steve said, "was that this was his way of saying to us 'A—you're Jewish. And B—this is a special day. For whatever reason I don't want to go to the synagogue, but I am going to take you to the most peaceful tranquil place to meditate for a half hour that I can think of . . . a dark place with the stars . . . ' Was that religious? He had that side of him. It was clearly spiritual. And that's how he expressed it. I've had a number of traditional Jews say, 'Oh, that's a terrible story.' I think it's a wonderful story, and I'm not embarrassed to tell it at all because that's who he was." The next Yom Kippur Steve Greenberg celebrated was as a freshman at Yale, when a girl he had met from Chicago, Myrna Katz, took him to services. They married and raised their two daughters as active Reform Jews.

Glenn never thought of himself as Jewish. He married a non-Jew and raised non-Jewish children. He said that his father had never told them that they were Jewish. Alva didn't start thinking about her Jewish heritage until she went away to the University of Pennsylvania. "And that was when I began to understand who Hank Greenberg was in the context of being Jewish and who the Gimbels were. . . . Philadelphia was where the Gimbels started and they were still a very big name there." She also married a non-Jew and did not raise her two sons and daughter as Jews. But when she sent her sons to boarding school, they had to choose a religion for chapel and one son said that he was Jewish and started attending Jewish services. Soon he informed his mother that he wanted to have a bar mitzvah.

"Fine," said Alva, who resolved to go to synagogue "to find out what was going to happen." That was the beginning of Alva's very limited Jewish education. At the 1995 bar mitzvah of her son, both her mother and her mother's sister told her that it was the first time they had been in a synagogue.

While Hank the Jewish icon would later marry a non-Jew, Caral the assimilated Gimbel married another Jew. Greenberg met Mary Jo Tarola, a pretty Howard Hughes discovery who starred in two B movies as Linda Douglas. After getting a role under her own name in a major feature, *Affair with a Stranger*, starring Jean Simmons and Victor Mature, she gave up acting. After seeing her films Hank never understood her lack of confidence in her abilities. He regarded himself as someone with only a small measure of talent who had become a star because he worked hard. Didn't Mary Jo have enough talent to become a movie star if she just worked at it? Didn't his sons, both of whom became successful businessmen, have enough talent so that with hard work they could be great athletes?

Steve tried to have a baseball career, even playing his father's position, first base, but in five years he could not make it out of the minors. He did reach the highest step, Class AAA, and even made it onto the roster of the Texas Rangers for one day, although he didn't play. He later became a deputy commissioner of baseball and a major figure in sports broadcasting as one of the creators of the ESPN Classic and other successful television sports innovations. Hank thought all three of his children had enough athletic talent for professional careers but lacked his desperation to get out of the Bronx. "They were raised a little different," he said. "A little easier. They had big hamburgers ready to be served to them and they had the television set in front of them."

Hank's attraction to Mary Jo gives an insight into his twelve-year marriage to Caral. Mary Jo was not at all like a Gimbel. Although she was not Jewish, in many ways she had more in common with Hank than Caral had. A plain-talking woman, she had an earthy manner and a lusty laugh. When Hank and Mary Jo got married in 1966, another ceremony before a justice of the peace, this time in Virginia, she told him that she wanted him to move to California. This was difficult for him. He loved New York and talked to the Veecks a lot about his decision. He complained that California was three hours behind the markets in New York, and that the people there were insincere. He would say to Mary Jo, "People say 'Let's have lunch' and you never see them again." But in 1972, when he gave in and moved with Mary Jo to Beverly Hills, he settled into some of the happiest years of his life. The southern California weather enabled him to play tennis almost every day, and he joined the Beverly Hills Tennis Club, with its pleasant outdoor courts. The club had been founded because the only previous club, the Los Angeles Tennis Club, had refused to accept as members either actors or Jews. So the Beverly Hills Club became the one for actors and Jews.

"The tennis club became his office," Steve Greenberg recalled. "Tennis and backgammon, and with the time change the markets were still open in New York [at the end of the day], so he could do some buying and selling on the phone." Steve became a player's agent living in Los Angeles, and father and son finally grew close. This was not only one of the great experiences of Steve's life but an unexpected fulfillment for Hank.

Whenever a client of Steve's came to town with his team, Steve would take him to the Beverly Hills Tennis Club to have lunch with Hank Greenberg. His father enjoyed talking to the young players. The actor Walter Matthau claimed that he didn't play tennis but had joined the tennis club just so that he could befriend his childhood hero, Hank Greenberg. After he moved to California, Greenberg kept in touch with few from the world of baseball except Veeck, who remained a close friend, and Ralph Kiner, whom he rarely saw. Mary Jo said that she once asked him why he didn't stay in touch with his old friend Joe DiMaggio, and Hank said, "If you said hello to him, he was stuck for an answer."

Hank Greenberg almost never talked about baseball anymore. He was more interested in the ideas stimulated by the history books and biographies he was constantly reading. He and Mary Jo became close to Karl Fleming, a *Newsweek* journalist noted for his coverage of the civil rights movement, and his wife, the writer Anne Taylor Fleming.

But though he had abandoned baseball, he would always be an athlete. Tennis became the center of his world, and he approached it with the same obsessive work ethic and quest to be the best that he had with the sport that made him famous. Anne Taylor Fleming said that though it was tough to play tennis against him, it was easier than playing on his side. "He meant to win," she said, "and if you let him down he was terrifying." A tireless competitor, he was determined to win at tennis, backgammon, anything he played. Fleming called him "the single most competitive person I ever met." When they weren't competing in games, he invented new ones, betting, for instance, that she couldn't finish a large meal because she was a small woman.

Hank also played tennis with Leonard Bierman, a lifelong player and Reform rabbi. About Greenberg's tennis game Bierman said, "He was a wily tennis player—by no means great but you always felt you were being psyched out. He lumbered and had a kind of stoop but he would find your weakness." Ten years younger than Greenberg, Bierman grew up in a small town near Detroit with few Jews and an active Ku Klux Klan. Greenberg was his hero. "There were other Jewish athletes," Bierman said. "But no one stood out like Hank Greenberg. He was the only example of muscular Jewish strength."

Greenberg loved to argue religion with Bierman, declaring

that religion caused violence, injustice, and suffering. Bierman would agree but point out that it also inspired great art and ideas. Greenberg would never concede this point. The extent of his religious observance was to stay away from the club on Yom Kippur. Nor did the ballplayer share the rabbi's progressive politics. Though usually a moderate Democrat, in 1968 Greenberg horrified Mary Jo by voting for Richard Nixon. Normally not quick to anger, he equated Bierman's criticism of Israel with anti-Semitism. Greenberg would accuse anyone who criticized Israel or defended Palestinians of being anti-Semitic. This was the one subject on which he tolerated no deviating points of view. In fact, his stance would be a factor in a bitter break with his son, Glenn, whose wife was a social worker with Palestinians. A fierce Zionist, Greenberg regarded Israel as the moral imperative of the Jewish people in the aftermath of the Holocaust, though he believed the new nation was doomed to fail. He thought it "unfair that Jews with so much talent and ingenuity have to make a homeland in a barren wasteland." Although he never visited Israel, not even when his children gave him a trip for his seventieth birthday, Greenberg donated money to build a tennis court in Israel. To Greenberg, like many Jews, Israel was a defense against anti-Semitism, and while he was not much interested in Jewish life, he had a great concern for protecting Jews from bigotry.

He began to work on his autobiography. Stephen had been urging him to tell his story, but Hank had always said that he wanted to wait until he did "something really great." Finally, though, he began to spend hours sitting by the pool at his home, dictating into a tape recorder.

Until the age of seventy-four, Greenberg played competitive tennis six days a week, winning pro-celebrity tournaments in Las Vegas in ninety-degree heat. He never needed his hips or knees replaced, like so many other athletes. He loved parties and celebrations. New Year's Eve, which turned into his birthday at midnight, was always a big event. One of his great pleasures was throwing a surprise party. "We all knew we were going to get one," said Anne Taylor Fleming, "and there was always good food. Everything he did was accompanied by copious and high-quality food." He became a connoisseur of fine wine and enjoyed martinis, but you could bring on his wrath by putting any garnish in a martini but a very small onion. He smoked excellent cigars and he liked caviar in "obscene amounts," as Mary Frances Veeck put it.

Every now and then a fan would infuriate him with the old myths. Once he was spotted by a fan in a Beverly Hills delicatessen where he and Mary Jo were eating. The fan said that he thought it was terrible that pitchers wouldn't throw him strikes because he was Jewish when he was going for Ruth's record. "Where the hell did you come up with that!" Greenberg exploded. "That is completely not true!" Of all the myths about Hank and his Jewishness, he particularly hated that one.

But he was not a man full of anger and frustration. He was a man whose life had worked out more or less the way he wanted it to. Fleming used the word *joyous* to describe him in his later years and said, "He had no dark ghosts." The grimly determined overachiever had come to peace with his life and his accomplishments.

In 1984 Hank Greenberg was seventy-three years old and had been fit all his life. His only memories of medical problems were his broken wrist in 1935 and elbow surgery in 1947. But that October he was told he had kidney cancer. He could not believe his body was failing him. Alva later theorized that the years of "ignoring" anti-Semitic harassments had taken a toll on his body, pointing out that Jackie Robinson had died of a heart attack at fifty-three. Hank stopped going to the club, saying he didn't want people to see him until he had fully recovered—as he was certain he would, according to Mary Jo. He forbade her to tell anyone, even their closest friends, that he was ill. He could not bear having people see him in a weakened condition. But soon he got even weaker, needing crutches to walk and suffering great pain. On September 4, 1986, Hank Greenberg died in his sleep at the age of seventy-five. Ralph Kiner, now a sports announcer, received the news while broadcasting from Fenway Park. "It was," he said, "the worst day of my life."

Hank had refused to discuss his funeral or burial, so Mary Jo, left to improvise, had Leonard Bierman perform a small Jewish funeral for the immediate family. She wasn't sure Hank would have wanted a Jewish service, but he had been fond of Bierman. Hank Greenberg was buried in a Jewish cemetery, the Hillside Memorial Park in Culver City, California, the resting place of Jack Benny, Eddie Cantor, and many other Jewish celebrities. His stone was inscribed, "Hank Greenberg—loved and admired by so many," with the image of a menorah carved over the words.

Two months later about three hundred people attended a memorial service at the Wadsworth Theatre on Wilshire Boulevard in West Los Angeles. Anything grander and Hank might have returned from the dead to refuse it. His friend Walter Matthau told of a story he had for years related about Greenberg's war experience. Hank, according to the story, faced down an anti-Semite at the port of embarkation, when he was about to be shipped overseas. One day Matthau related the story to Greenberg, who insisted that it had never happened. Matthau was crushed because he loved the story; he asked whether his friend would mind if he continued telling it. Greenberg, ever gracious, agreed.

Baseball alone could never explain Hank Greenberg's life. He was a man with a strong sense of who he was and what he wanted from life. He loved the game, he loved the competition, and he even loved the simple act of hitting fly balls for hours, trying to make each swing a little better than the one before. But baseball was not the goal of Greenberg's life; it was just a tool for achieving his goal. At the memorial service, Ralph Kiner recounted some of Hank's accomplishments in baseball and then said, "All these things were there but they're not the important things, because Hank Greenberg was a man that, if you were fortunate enough to be around, you never forgot him."

Steve said, "Thirty years after he finished playing, in the seventies into the eighties, he'd show me his mail. He'd get thirty letters a day. People asking for autographs. And everyone with a story. . . . It almost embarrassed him. For a long time in his life, he wasn't comfortable with it. By the end of his life he got very comfortable, and I think he came to understand that it was important."

As he had with Walter Matthau, Hank realized that people needed to tell the stories; he shouldn't take those stories away. He said in his autobiography, "It's a strange thing. When I was playing I resented being singled out as a Jewish ballplayer, period. I'm not sure why or when I changed, because I'm still not a particularly religious person. Lately, though, I find myself wanting to be remembered not only as a great ballplayer, but even more as a great Jewish ballplayer. I realize now, more than I used to, how important a part I played in the lives of a generation of Jewish kids who grew up in the thirties." He had come to understand, difficult for a man of his modesty, that he had a place in history. He had never aspired to anything so grand. At his core he was just the son of immigrants trying to move beyond their world and achieve a prosperous American life.

Still, he told the American Jewish Committee, "If I'm an example, I'm only an example in the way I conduct my life. I want to conduct my life in an exemplary manner."

"Set the example of being a good citizen," he said, "live by the Ten Commandments, and if that sets a good example,

I think that's fine." While he was not about to observe the Sabbath, he did honor his mother and father, even as he had left them far behind in the Bronx and had grown even more distant from his brothers and sister. He was generous and compassionate. Before he died he left an eloquent love letter to his wife, telling her not to grieve because he had lived "a wonderful life" and part of it was his good fortune to have shared twenty-five years with her. As Anne Taylor Fleming said, "He thought he had done what he was supposed to with his life."

In *Humboldt's Gift*, Saul Bellow writes, "He blew his talent and his health and reached home, the grave, in a dusty slide." That wasn't the way Hank Greenberg played the game or reached home. In fact, after he retired he confessed that he had studied how to steal home but had never had the nerve to try. The Greenberg way was to slam one over the left field wall, knocking it out of the park, and then lope around the bases, looking too big for the diamond, head dropped low as if embarrassed or, possibly, taking a gracious bow.

Epilogue

————◆·◆·◆————

More Holy Days

Possibly I believed only gentiles
And blonds could be left-handed
—Robert Pinsky, "The Night Game"

IN 1954, game five of the World Series between the Indians
and the Giants was scheduled for Yom Kippur and Cleveland
star hitter Al Rosen, one of the best Jewish players of all time,
announced that he would not play. The Indians' general manager, Hank Greenberg, understood. But the Giants swept the Indians in four games and the Series never made it to Yom Kippur.

Rosen may have been influenced by the fact that, growing
up a Jewish kid in Miami, he idolized Greenberg, and he remembered the 1934 incident, when he was a ten-year-old.
Rosen had experienced enough anti-Semitism in baseball to
consider changing his name to Ross. Later he completely re-
versed his thinking and thought that he would have preferred
Rosenberg. Greenberg had a lot to do with that change in

thinking. The Indians' general manager infuriated Rosen with his toughness in negotiating contracts, but the younger player always credited Greenberg with having paved a path for Jews in baseball.

Other players have sat out important games in observance of the Jewish holidays, but the only time such a decision has caused the sort of excitement that Greenberg's occasioned was the 1965 World Series. Brooklyn-born Sandy Koufax was the Dodgers' star pitcher, one of the great pitchers of baseball history, the only other Jewish player to achieve Greenberg's level of acclaim, the only other Jewish Hall of Famer. In 1965 Yom Kippur set the scene for one of his great tour de force performances. Pitchers don't play every day, so skipping a day for a Jewish holiday is usually not as disruptive to the team as it would be with a key everyday player like Greenberg. That is, unless the pitcher happens to be his team's ace starting pitcher in a World Series that opens on Yom Kippur.

In the 1960s, when starting pitchers routinely were given three days between starts (today four days is standard) and a seven-game World Series was played over nine days, the best starter, by pitching game one, would have his normal rest before pitching game four and then, if necessary, game seven. Koufax did not pitch on Rosh Hashanah or the first night of Passover, and he would not pitch on Yom Kippur. Luckily for the Dodgers, the team had one of the best pitching rotations in baseball history. The number two pitcher was six-foot-six-inch right-hander Don Drysdale, like Koufax a future Hall of Famer —and unlike the gentlemanly Koufax, notorious for firing deadly fastballs high and inside.

Drysdale pitched game one, but the Minnesota Twins hit him so hard that he was taken out of the game in the third inning with the score at 7–0. While Koufax atoned for his sins in a Minneapolis synagogue or stayed in his hotel room, depending on which account you read, the Twins won 8–2. With Yom

Kippur over, Koufax pitched game two and allowed only one earned run in six innings, but the Dodger batters, defense, and relief pitchers let him down. The Twins won 5–0 to take a two-games-to-none lead in the series, having beaten the best pitchers the Dodgers had.

But with the Series moving to Los Angeles after a day off, Claude Osteen, a crafty pitcher who might have been the ace on a lesser team, pitched a shutout in game three as the Dodgers won 4–0. Then it was Drysdale's turn again, and he decisively won game four 7–2, striking out 11 batters. For game five a rested Koufax was back. He gave up only four singles and struck out 10, pitching the full nine innings and winning 7–0. It was the kind of performance the Dodgers counted on Koufax to deliver.

After the Dodgers' three victories in Los Angeles, the Series returned to Minneapolis. The Dodgers needed only one more win to clinch the Series and prove that Koufax's religious day off had not hurt them at all. But Osteen was less effective this time around, and the Twins won game six 5–1.

With the teams tied at three wins each, game seven would decide the Series one way or another: it was the last game of the season, with no reason to hold back. If Koufax had pitched game 1 on Yom Kippur, he would have been fully rested now and available for the most critical game. But because of his observance, he had had only two days' rest since pitching nine innings. Drysdale, who had 23 pitching victories during the season to Koufax's major league–leading 26, had had a full three days off. But the Dodgers decided on Koufax, who again pitched all nine innings, again struck out 10 batters, shut the Twins out on three hits, and won the game 2–0. On a mere two days' rest from a complete game, Koufax pitched one of the greatest game seven performances in World Series history.

That was a big week for the Jews. It was happy, it was fun. People celebrated. But it didn't carry the emotional impact of the Yom Kippur in 1934, when Greenberg decided not to play.

Koufax's victory was just a great day. It wasn't a response to Henry Ford, Father Coughlin, and Adolf Hitler.

It is in part thanks to Hank Greenberg that today's Jewish players no longer face the harassment that he did. Kevin Youkilis, a Cincinnati-born Jew who has made a reputation as a flawless infielder and timely hitter for the Red Sox since 2004, has said that he experienced little anti-Semitism in baseball. "Teammates drop the usual jokes. We joke about all ethnic backgrounds. Dominicans, whatever. It's not along the lines of hatred. Today people travel more and know more about cultures and know how to joke about it. The hatred is from ignorance." Youkilis did play one Rosh Hashanah, using the old 1934 Greenberg argument that you were allowed to do things that you loved on the Jewish New Year. Few people cared. Shawn Green of the Dodgers, Art Shamsky of the Mets, and several other Jewish players have played or not played games on the Jewish holidays, with little attention paid to their decisions.

Greenberg's battles in baseball are over. But Greenberg's dreams had always gone far beyond baseball. He used to talk about a world in which religions didn't separate people. That separation, he frequently explained, was the reason he didn't like religion. He liked to imagine a world without bigotry. Kevin Youkilis can imagine it too. Youkilis said, "The great thing about today is that people are more educated and hopefully eventually everybody will be educated and the whole thing will go away." But baseball players tend to be optimists. How else could you step out on a field 162 times a year, convinced each time that you are going to win?

BIBLIOGRAPHY

Oral History and Interviews

Interview with Hank Greenberg, American Jewish Committee Oral History Collection, Dorot Jewish Division, New York Public Library, Astor, Lenox and Tilden Foundations.

The author interviewed the following people: Morris Barrett, Leonard Bierman, Ron Blomberg, Reeve Brenner, Harriet Coleman, Anne Taylor Fleming, Alva Greenberg, Dana Greenberg, Mary Jo DeCicco Greenberg, Stephen Greenberg, Herbert Greenwald, Bernard Karlin, Al Kirchenstein, Allan Lackner, Martin Mayer, Lester Pashkin, Jerry Reinsdorf, Rachel Robinson, Art Shamsky, Eliot Sharlit, Robert Steinberg, Mary Frances Veeck, Julius Wolk, and Kevin Youkilis.

Web Sites

The Internet is an endless source of erroneous information, on baseball as on other topics, but it also has a few very good sources.

www.baseball-almanac.com
www.baseballhalloffame.org
www.baseball-reference.com

Books

Alexander, Charles C. *Breaking the Slump: Baseball in the Depression Era.* New York: Columbia University Press, 2002.

Angell, Roger. *Five Seasons: A Baseball Companion.* New York: Simon and Schuster, 1972.

Auker, Elden, with Tom Keegan. *Sleeper Cars and Flannel Uniforms: A Lifetime of Memories from Striking Out the Babe to Teeing Up with the President.* Chicago: Triumph, 2001.

Chafets, Zev. *Cooperstown Confidential: Heroes, Rogues, and the Inside Story of the Baseball Hall of Fame.* New York: Bloomsbury, 2009.

Cohen, Irwin J. *Echoes of Detroit's Jewish Communities.* Laingsburg, MI: City Vision, 2003.

Curran, William. *Mitts: A Celebration of the Art of Fielding.* New York: William Morrow, 1985.

Detroit News. They Earned Their Stripes: The Detroit Tigers All-Time Team. United States: Sports Publishing, 2001.

Diner, Hasia R. *A New Promised Land: A History of Jews in America.* New York: Oxford University Press, 2000.

Dinnerstein, Leonard. *Anti-Semitism in America.* New York: Oxford University Press, 1994.

Greenberg, Hank. *The Story of My Life.* Ed. Ira Berkow. New York: Times Books, 1989.

Gurock, Jeffrey S. *Judaism's Encounter with American Sports.* Bloomington: Indiana University Press, 2005.

Hample, Zack. *Watching Baseball Smarter: A Professional Fan's Guide for Beginners, Semi-Experts, and Deeply Serious Geeks.* New York: Vintage, 2007.

Howe, Irving. *World of Our Fathers: The Journey of the East European Jews to America and the Life They Found and Made.* New York: Harcourt Brace Jovanovich, 1976.

Kaiser, David. *Epic Season: The 1948 American League Pennant Race.* Amherst: University of Massachusetts Press, 1998.

Koppett, Leonard. *The Thinking Fan's Guide to Baseball.* Rev. ed. Toronto: SportClassic, 2004.

Leavy, Jane. *Sandy Koufax: A Lefty's Legacy.* New York: Harper-Collins, 2002.

Levine, Peter. *A. G. Spalding and the Rise of Baseball: The Promise of American Sport.* New York: Oxford University Press, 1985.

————. *Ellis Island to Ebbets Field: Sport and the American Jewish Experience.* New York: Oxford University Press, 1992.

Lynn, Erwin. *The Jewish Baseball Hall of Fame.* New York: Shapolsky, 1986.

Mehno, John. *The Chronicle of Baseball: A Century of Major League Action.* London: Carlton, 2000.

Moore, Deborah Dash. *At Home in America: Second Generation New York Jews.* New York: Columbia University Press, 1981.

Postal, Bernard, Jesse Silver, and Roy Silver. *Encyclopedia of Jews in Sports.* New York: Bloch, 1965.

Rampersad, Arnold. *Jackie Robinson: A Biography.* New York: Alfred A. Knopf, 1997.

Reiss, Stephen A., ed. *Sports and the American Jew.* Syracuse: Syracuse University Press, 1998.

Roth, Philip. *Reading Myself and Others.* New York: Farrar, Straus and Giroux, 1961.

Shamsky, Art, with Barry Zeman. *The Magnificent Seasons: How the Jets, Mets, and Knicks Made Sports History and Uplifted a City and the Country.* New York: St. Martin's, 2004.

Smith, Red. *Red Smith on Baseball: The Game's Greatest Writer on the Game's Greatest Years.* Chicago: Ivan R. Dee, 2000.

Snyder, Brad. *A Well-Paid Slave: Curt Flood's Fight for Free Agency in Professional Sports.* New York: Plume, 2006.

Turner, Frederick. *When the Boys Came Back: Baseball and 1946.* New York: Henry Holt, 1996.

Veeck, Bill, with Ed Linn. *Veeck as in Wreck: The Autobiography of Bill Veeck.* Chicago: University of Chicago Press, 1962.

Wenger, Beth S. *New York Jews and the Great Depression: Uncertain Promise.* New Haven: Yale University Press, 1996.

Will, George F. *Bunts: Curt Flood, Camden Yards, Pete Rose, and Other Reflections on Baseball.* New York: Scribner, 1998.

ACKNOWLEDGMENTS

THANKS TO my great agent, Charlotte Sheedy, to my friend Art Shamsky for all his help, to Susan Birnbaum for all her good work, to Ira Berkow for his generous advice, and to Stephen Greenberg and all of the Greenberg family for their openness and cooperation. I also want to thank Rachel Robinson and Della Britton Baeza of the Jackie Robinson Foundation for their help and insights. Thanks to Nancy Miller for helping me shape this book. Thanks also to Ileene Smith for her guidance and editing and to Steven Zipperstein for his advice. And a special thanks to my wonderful friend Rubye Monet for answering all my Yiddish questions, to my good friend George Gibson for answering baseball questions, and to Tim Wiles and Freddy Berowski at the library of the Baseball Hall of Fame in Cooperstown who answered even more baseball questions.

INDEX

Aaron, Hank, xiii
Adams, John Quincy, 53
African Americans. *See* racism;
  and specific individuals
Aleichem, Shalom, 8
Allen, Harold, 84
Allen, Sidney, 84
All-Star team of *1937*, 35
American Jewish Committee, Green-
  berg interview: on anti-Semitism,
  71, 86–87; on baseball as escape, 51,
  126; on his approach to practice, 37;
  on his isolation as a Jew in baseball,
  75; on his Jewish identity, 126–27;
  on learning Hebrew, 34, 126; on
  setting a good example, 143–44
Andrews Sisters, 80–81
Angell, Roger, 79
Angels (Los Angeles), 132–33
Anson, Cap, 118
anti-immigration laws, 54
anti-Semitism (generally): in the

1930s, 9, 55–61, 79–80; in basketball, 64; concern that celebrity
  would provoke, 12, 52–53, 80; in
  Detroit, 11, 56–59; Ginsberg on,
  52; and the Greenberg myth, 12;
  Greenberg's defense of Israel, 140;
  Greenberg's popularity and, 79–80;
  history of American anti-Semitism,
  53–56; and Jewish boxers, 30–31;
  and Jewish immigration, 23–24;
  Jewish stereotypes, 16–17; in New
  York, 29, 33, 44, 65; soldiers and,
  99; after World War II, 108. *See also*
  anti-Semitism in baseball
anti-Semitism in baseball: Cohen and,
  46, 64; early days, 22–23; Ford on,
  60–61; and Greenberg's attempt to
  break Ruth's record, 92–93; Greenberg's experience of, 66, 116; Greenberg's response to, xii–xiv, 71–72,
  85–87, 96, 116–17, 119, 121; hotel
  rooms refused to Jewish players, 75;

anti-Semitism in baseball (*continued*):
name-calling and baiting, 64,
71–72, 82, 85; from opposing teams,
71–72, 82, 85, 96, 108–9; and play-
ers' names, 14–15, 43–44, 64,
145–46; today, 148; after World
War II, 108–9. *See also* anti-
Semitism (generally)
Aparicio, Luis, 131
Arnovich, Morris, 75, 79, 98, 101, 108
At Home in America (Moore), 69
athletic centers, Jewish, 24–25, 30
Athletics. *See* Philadelphia Athletics
Attell, Abe, 32
Auker, Eldon, 6–7, 85–86

Bagby, Jim, 116–17
Bailey, Josiah, 99
Baker, Jesse, 43
Baltimore Orioles, 23
Barrett, Morris (Berkowitz), 14–15
baseball: assimilation through, 24,
25–26; ball, 36; batting average, 2;
designated hitter, 133; ethnic prejudice in, 64; first base (position), 87;
Greenberg in management, 129–33;
home run history and popularity,
77–79; Jewish attitudes toward, 16,
37–38, 42, 50–51; and the Jewish
holidays, 2–3 (*see also* Rosh Hashanah; Yom Kippur); Jewish owners,
22–23; Jewish players before Greenberg, 14, 20–23, 43–44; marriage
and, 113; pennant races, 3; players
in WWII military, 101–2, 105–8;
players' moral character, xiv; racism
in, xii–xiii, 118–23, 129–30;
regular-season inter-league games,
133; reserve clause, 115, 122–23;
salary negotiations, 49–50; strike
zone, 128; umpires, 93–94; in urban
New York neighborhoods, 29–30;
Veeck's attempts to integrate,
129–30; during World War II, 102;
after World War II, 103–4. *See also*
anti-Semitism in baseball; *and
specific teams and individuals*

basketball, 30, 40, 41
batting average, 2. *See also* Greenberg,
Hank (as baseball player)
Beaumont, Texas, Class A team, 70,
72–73
Beazley, Johnny, 102
"Bei Mir Bistu Shein" (Secunda and
Jacobs song), 80–81
Bellow, Saul, 17, 28, 50, 144
Berenson, Bernard, 30
Berenson, Senda, 30
Berg, Moe, 44–45, 54, 75, 76, 102
Berg, Sam, 44
Berkow, Ira, 29, 110
Berkowitz, Morris (Barrett), 14–15
Berman, Bob, 44
Bernstein, Jack, 31
Beverly Hills Tennis Club, 138
Bialik, Haim Nachman, 31
Bierman, Leonard, 139–40, 142
Blady, Ken, 31
Blomberg, Ron, 133
Bohne, Sam, 43
Bonds, Barry, 90
Bonham, Tiny, 98
Borowy, Hank, 105
Bostick, Henry, 43
Boston Braves, 130
Boston Red Sox: 1934 Rosh Hashanah
game, 4; Jewish players, 45, 148;
Krichell and, 47; vs. Tigers (1939),
116; during World War II, 107.
See also Fenway Park; Williams, Ted
boxers, Jewish, 11–12, 19–20, 30–32
Brandeis, Louis, 53, 54, 56–57
Bridges, Tommy, 88
Brooklyn Dodgers: and Robinson, xiii,
118–21; during World War II, 102.
See also Los Angeles Dodgers; *and
specific players*
Brown, K. O., 31
Brown, Lloyd, 73
Brown, Tommy, 102
Brown, Warren, 105
Browns. *See* St. Louis Browns
Buchwald, Art, 89
Buffalo Bisons, 46

INDEX

Doby, Larry, xiii, 130
Dodgers. *See* Brooklyn Dodgers;
 Los Angeles Dodgers
Donald, Atley, 98–99
Douglas, Linda, 137. *See also* Green-
 berg, Mary Jo (wife of H.G.)
Drysdale, Don, 146, 147
Dubuc, Jean, 66

Eisenstat, Harry, 76, 87, 101
Emerson, Ralph Waldo, xii
Evans, Billy, 114
Evansville Hubs, 70–71
Ewing, Reuben (Cohen), 22, 43

Feinberg, Eddie, 75
Feller, Bob, 76
Fenway Park (Boston), 91
Fishel, Leo, 21
Five Seasons (Angell), 79
Fleming, Anne Taylor, 139, 141, 144
Fleming, Karl, 139
Flood, Curt, 122–23, 129
Ford, Henry, 57–58, 60–61, 63
Fosdick, Harry Emerson, 55–56
Foxx, Jimmie, 35, 92
Frankfurter, Felix, 53
Franklin, Rabbi Leo, 4–5, 58
Freedman, Andrew, 22–23
Freeman, Julius, 21
Frisch, Frankie, 40

Gaedel, Eddie, 127–28
Garfield, John (Julius Garfinkle), 80
Gebert, Konstanty, xii–xiii
Gedeon, Elmer, 105–6
Gehrig, Lou: 1937 All-Star team, 35;
 records, 88, 90, 96; and the Yankees,
 40, 47–49, 67, 88
Gehringer, Charlie: 1934 season, 2, 4;
 1937 season, 35, 88; as player, 1, 2;
 and the rookie Greenberg, 63
Germany (Nazi era). *See* Nazism and
 Nazi Germany
Giants. *See* New York Giants
Gimbel, Bernard, and family, 110,
 111–12, 132

Gimbel, Caral. *See* Greenberg, Caral
 Gimbel
Ginsberg, Ruth Bader, 52
Goddard, Paulette, 80
Goldberg, Arthur, 122–23
Golden Boy (film), 102–3
Goldenberg, Emmanuel, 80
Goldman, David J., 100
Goldstein, Izzy, 22, 26, 41, 75
Gompers, Samuel, 30
Gonzalez, Mike, 45
Goodman, Jake, 21
Göring, Hermann, 56
Goslin, Goose, 2
Graham, Frank, 105
Gray, Pete, 102
Great Contemporaries (Churchill), 60
Green, Shawn, 148
Greenberg, Alva (daughter of H.G.):
 childhood, 131, 134, 135; on her
 father, 125, 134; and her Jewish
 heritage, 136–37; on her parents,
 111, 132
Greenberg, Benjamin (brother of
 H.G.), 14, 29, 50, 64, 69
Greenberg, Caral Gimbel (wife of
 H.G.): as art collector, 112, 126;
 courtship and wedding, 110–12,
 125; divorce, 131–32; Hank's second
 wife contrasted with, 138; in Pittsburgh, 115; son born, 114; tennis
 played, 129; third marriage, 137
Greenberg, Dana (journalist), 101
Greenberg, David (father of H.G.):
 in Crotona Park, 32; Hank taken to
 major league game, 40; and Hank's
 baseball playing, 38, 41–42, 49, 50;
 and Hank's college career, 41–42,
 49, 50; on Hank's decision not to
 play on Yom Kippur, 13, 82; and
 Hank's major league career, 69,
 81–82, 83; immigration and marriage, 28–29; loved by Hank, 144;
 Orthodoxy, 33–34, 82, 135; work
 ethic, 37
Greenberg, Eric Rolfe (novelist), 26,
 62

World War II service, 102, 108;
after World War II, 104, 108
Williamson, Ned, 78
Wise, Rabbi Stephen, 50–60
Wohlgelernter, Eli, 51
Wolk, Julius, 14, 32–34, 36, 38
World Series: 1906 series, 78; 1924
series, 67–68; 1934 series, 8–13, 10,
87, 147; 1935 series, 82, 87; 1940
series, 96; 1942 series, 102; 1945
series, 104–5; 1948 series, 130; 1954
series, 145–46; 1965 series, 146–48;
and the Jewish holidays, 1, 2–3,
8–13, 126, 146–48; not attended by
Bronx residents, 41; pennant races
and, 3
World War II: baseball players' military service, 98–102, 105–8, 142;
draft registration, 96–97; events
preceding, 59–60, 89; the Holo-

caust, 127, 140. *See also* Nazism and
Nazi Germany

Yankee Stadium, 36, 39–40, 48–49, 88
Yankees. *See* New York Yankees
Yekl: A Tale of the New York Ghetto
(Cahan), 16
Yiddish, 80–81
Yom Kippur: 1934 World Series and, 8–
13, 126; 1935 World Series and, 12–
13, 82; 1954 World Series and, 145–
46; 1965 World Series and, 146–48;
about, 8; planetarium visited, 136;
tennis not played on, 140
York, Rudy, 96, 104, 113
Youkilis, Kevin, 148
Young Men's Hebrew Association
(YMHA), 24–25, 30

Zionism, 18, 80, 140

JEWISH LIVES is a major series of interpretive
biography designed to illuminate the imprint of eminent Jewish
figures upon literature, religion, philosophy, politics, cultural and
economic life, and the arts and sciences. Subjects are paired with
authors to elicit lively, deeply informed books that explore the
breadth and complexity of Jewish experience
from antiquity through the present.

Jewish Lives is a partnership of Yale University Press
and the Leon D. Black Foundation.

Anita Shapira and Steven J. Zipperstein
are series editors.